# FRANCE,
# THE SOUL OF A JOURNEY

# FRANCE, THE SOUL OF A JOURNEY

R J ODONNELL

Matador
9 Priory Business Park
Kibworth Beauchamp
Leicestershire LE8 0RX, UK
Tel: (+44) 116 279 2299
Fax: (+44) 116 279 2277
Email: books@troubador.co.uk
Web: www.troubador.co.uk/matador

ISBN 978-1783065-417

British Library Cataloguing in Publication Data.
A catalogue record for this book is available from the British Library.

Typeset in Aldine by Troubador Publishing Ltd
Printed and bound in the UK by TJ International, Padstow, Cornwall

**Matador** is an imprint of Troubador Publishing Ltd

"EVERY MAN HAS TWO COUNTRIES:
HIS OWN AND FRANCE."

ATTRIBUTED TO THOMAS JEFFERSON

# CHAPTER 1

Arriving in Calais reminded me of my first trip to France when I took off on my own to Paris with just a single address in my pocket. Back then all sorts of prospects spread out before me in a dreamy haze. I hadn't even planned where I would spend the night. I didn't know what a bad idea that was. Bad ideas belonged to the world of adults. Adults created their own needs by thinking they needed them, like arrangements for instance. How charmingly half-baked I was. Time sure alters things. Once cooked fully, life has a habit of forming a hard crust around the soft dough of wide-eyed youthfulness. These days I wouldn't stir outside my door without allowing for every conceivable risk and, indeed, some not so conceivable. Sometimes I'd love to shed all that good sense I once managed so wonderfully without. But I bet if I tried that, things wouldn't happen with the same lightness as they did then.

Back then I got a job minding two children with a family in Paris. I understood just about enough French to know that the youngest, Delphine, a feisty five-year-old, told her mother anew each morning how little she liked me, that she preferred Emily, my predecessor. I let on not to understand but that only made me look dim, which, combined with being unloved made for a poor mixture. Delphine had her way in the end, and her mother, who used to kiss me on both cheeks each morning, was plotting behind her hugs to find someone else for the job. I found out when I took a phone call from a young woman speaking strongly accented English. Could I give Madame Le Clerc a message, she asked.

"And what is the message?" I asked helpfully.

1

"Tell her Ana is not interested in the job as au pair."

And I did. I delivered that message as meekly as if it had been in my favour.

"I'm so worried about you going off on your own," Madame Le Clerc said, half crying, when I said I was going to join my friends in Jersey.

"Don't worry, I couldn't meet anyone worse than you," I said. Actually, I didn't say it. But I thought it with a vengeance.

These days when I'm in France, in this country of rolling hills, sunshine and gastronomy, I can hardly believe it's the same place that I viewed so long with the weight of au pair baggage. These memories had well dispersed that day we arrived in Calais: Steve, Treasa, Declan and I. Our holiday began eagerly, perhaps not quite the youthful dreamy kind that I experienced on my first trip, but exciting enough considering the hard crust of adulthood had by now securely encased us.

Steve is great fun. To get a flavour of him is to see him at a party, getting the singing going and drawing even the most reticent into the enjoyment. He says that a long time ago, when he thought of all the things he could worry about, he decided not to worry at all. I reckon that someone who has made that leap in attitude is the ideal journeying companion. He is good at lightening sulks and broodings, and on holidays that particular skill is much called upon.

Treasa brings a gust of passion to the group. She says that being burdened by neither the practical nor the technical (she claims that she can just about tie her laces) allows her to take a jaunty approach to life. She all but bursts into hymn at the most ordinary of things, and her lyrical outlook contrasts comically with Declan's take on life.

Declan is very rational, good with plans, maps, directions, proportions, those sort of things. Often, while the rest of us are chatting, his head is stuck in a map. I sometimes think he must feel very bored for the rest of the year, when he knows exactly where he's going. A few years ago he was whipped off in an ambulance in the middle of the night with a chest pain. The paramedic kept asking him if he knew where he was, to test if he was still conscious, I presume. But he told him, not only did he know where he was, he knew the exact route they were taking to the hospital, even though he was lying on a stretcher. The question was not repeated. Maybe the paramedic was afraid to ask in case the patient would suggest a better route.

No one has told me whether I bring any special quality to the group, and I don't intend to ask in case someone is cruel enough to reveal some truth I'd be better off not knowing.

As we drove off the ferry in Calais, Treasa said, "There's something about ports and boats that bring to mind half-remembered nursery rhymes of seafaring and mariners of old." She didn't notice the side-glance Declan gave her, and she went on: "I just love the double clang of the ferry's ramp against the harbour's edge as you drive into a foreign land."

I was sharing her joy. It's one of those instants of raw exhilaration – the different accents, the road signs in a language that isn't yours, shops with strange-sounding family names, driving on the "wrong" side of the road, which makes you feel you're going to spend time in a place where the rules of everyday life are about to be subverted.

Declan wasn't wistful at all. He was muttering that the journey would have been so much easier by plane. His idea of a holiday is to go, in a mere few hours, from warm clothing to a destination where you can dine beneath a tree or sip your drink outside in the fading light until midnight without putting on an extra layer. Treasa has a name for this kind of point-to-point travelling – arrivalism. Real travel is a slow process, she believes.

"To go through the soul of a journey, it has to be felt from start to finish; anything else is cutting through its heart," she said. "It's like the difference between slow cooking and microwave food."

"OK, OK, point made," Declan said grumpily.

It wasn't really a struggle to get his agreement, because essentially Declan is easy-going, and besides, he's blessed with enough logic to know that with Treasa disagreeing with him and two more weighing in on her side, the odds were stacked against him. Besides, having the car meant that he could bring back some local wine so maybe he wasn't so very opposed to this slow method of travel after all.

My reason for going overland was not as lyrical as Treasa's. I hate heights. Three steps of a ladder is the limit of my upwards journey, maybe four if I'm in an especially adventurous mood. I've tried to overcome it. I've read every book in sight about the fear of flying. I did a course that was supposed to have me flying without a care in the world. It involved a simulated flight on a vibrating platform, with a helmet-like thing on your head and an image of the inside of a plane before your eyes. The patient woman who was directing the course asked me why I hadn't broken into a cold sweat like I normally do when I'm on a real plane. I told her that, with all due respect to her power of transformability, I knew I wasn't on a genuine flight. I was as conscious of my whereabouts as Declan was in the ambulance that night he was hauled off to hospital.

Steve doesn't care much about flying either. He loves anything to do with the sea. His favourite pastime is sailing.

When he lost the argument, Declan said wryly: "OK, let's slow-cook the trip then. Let's drive through the soul of the journey."

With all our differences, compromise was going to be much in demand if we wanted to come back on speaking terms.

We had booked into the Ibis hotel in Abbeville for the night. Abbeville is about an hour's drive from Calais. There were few cars on the road and it was delightful to drive at a leisurely pace in the slanting rays of evening sun. The Ibis hotel chain is pretty standard but the one in Abbeville has a certain "unstandardness" about it. When you open your bedroom window you look down on farmland, a tilled field or a swaying crop, which makes it very rural.

Abbeville is a popular stopover. A bus was offloading its cargo in the car park. There was so much buzz in the hotel that we stayed in the lounge, just for one drink. But one turned into quite a few. It didn't take many people to fill the small hotel lounge. The table was

4

finding it hard to accommodate all the glasses. You had to take care it was your own glass and not your neighbour's you were sipping from, and as evening stretched giddily into night and the drinks totted up, identifying your glass became hazier. We mingled with a coach tour from Wales who were on their way home, and in the warm atmosphere we began to feel like friends. By the end of the evening we were exchanging addresses and promising to look up one another the next time we went their way or they came ours.

A quietly spoken Welshman with rimless glasses droned off a dozen or so places they had visited: Rennes, Brest, Carnac and a few others that I didn't catch. A stern-looking woman beside him with tightly cut grey hair, who looked like a retired teacher, asked me if I knew what the lights beaming at the edge of the horizon were. I hadn't noticed them until then. They were filling the sky with light, as if something festive was going on in the distance. She told us she had read four books of fiction during her holiday, in English translation, three of which were by French author, Émile Zola. She carried them all in her bag, though her son had offered to lighten her load with an E-reader. No. Emphatically no, she had told him. She liked the feel of a book. "Sure," he answered, "I do too. But could you not compromise for your holidays?"

No. She liked to mark margins, she told us, add in her own comments and even rewrite some passages that could have been done better.

She said that the lights in the distance reminded her of the opening scene of Zola's *Germinal*.

"The setting must have been quite near here. Have you read it?" she asked, peering at us over her glasses, as if she was asking if we had done our homework.

I had seen the film. Not quite as good.

"Do you remember when Etienne trudged in the pitch black across the flat beet fields, when he spotted the lights of the coalmine in the horizon? Do you remember that?" she demanded.

Even if I couldn't I would have pretended to.

We decided to ask the receptionist about the lights.

"What? Flashing lights? Where? In your room, is it?"

Oh dear. How things get altered in translation. When she finally spotted the subject of all the fuss, she just shrugged her shoulders. The French excel at the shrug.

"It's useless talking to young people about books. They just don't read nowadays. It's all television and computer games," the "retired teacher" continued despairingly, as if there was a connection between the receptionist's disinterest and the decline in reading.

Next morning was like a different world, the enigma of the flashing lights washed clean in the early morning sun. The source of the lights turned out to be no more than a wind farm, not the festive occasion we had imagined. The people whom the lounge was hard pressed to accommodate hours earlier had gone their separate ways to catch their trains and ferries. I bet they never gave us another thought, much less look us up in the future. Staff whirred around getting the rooms ready for the next arrivals. My own thoughts were on breakfast.

I love the crunchy flavour of French breakfast – the assorted jams, the croissants, the crusty bread smelling deliciously of the *boulangerie*. You're never far from a bakery in France, no matter how small the village. The baker begins the day in the small hours of morning, to make sure his produce is freshly ready for breakfast. It's as unthinkable to eat yesterday's bread in France as it is to read last week's TV guide. An assortment of breads, each one bearing its own name, are formed into twists, loops and turns and shaped into veritable works of art.

There's one part of the French breakfast I still feel a nostalgia for – the broad-rimmed bowls they used to serve tea and coffee in. Your face would disappear as you went in for each mouthful. Nowadays they use cups with handles like the rest of us. Pity. It's just another symbol of the French way of life that has gone under the globalised steamroller, like the beret or the bidet. You see fewer and fewer Frenchmen wearing berets these days and as for the bidet, French bathrooms look just the same as everyone else's now. You'll only remember the bidet and all its mistaken uses if you are of a certain age – *d'un certain âge* – as they discreetly call middle age in French. Up until the seventies nearly all French bathrooms were fitted with a bidet, but by the close of the twentieth century they had become a rarity. I wonder what that says about the French?

Steve says it's all this EU commonality – common agricultural policy, common smoking ban, common currency, common bathrooms that are intent on making us all equally common.

We were soon ready to leave. We had parked the car the previous evening under a silver birch in the hotel car park and it was twinkling in the morning light as we put our bags in the boot. In a nearby field the green blades of an unfamiliar crop were bowing in the breeze. Their nodding agreeableness swayed in tune with the country friendliness of the area. I delayed the others by going back to the hotel to ask the dark-haired woman who was clearing off the tables what the crop was called.

"*Colza,*" she told me. When I made a note of the name she looked at it and said "*Très bien*" like a teacher would, for having written it correctly. The French often encourage you like that when you get something right: *Très bien* – it sounds like an appreciation of a foreigner making an effort in their language and it has a sweetness about it. The English translation of *colza* is rape seed.

Steve had suggested that we shouldn't leave Abbeville without having a look around the town. He had been doing some reading on the Crusades and he said Abbeville had been an assembly point for the First Crusaders. That lit up our interest.

# CHAPTER 2

Abbeville had all the pleasantness of a rural town. It opened out towards the surrounding fields and sloping hills but the centre looked a bit forlorn. A new square had been inserted when they rebuilt the town centre after the gutting it suffered in the German bombardment of 20 May 1940. This date became fixed in local lore when eight centuries of ancient houses, which once formed the narrow streets of Abbeville, crashed into debris. The inferno lasted nine terrible hours and when the roaring sirens died down and the locals tiptoed out of their cellars and hideouts they learned that Belgium, Holland and Luxembourg had been overrun. Soon a line of refugees who had made the trip across the border on bikes, wagons and cars loaded with every moveable object, provided them with more immediate proof.

The centre, a square and a straight row of new housing, Declan said was like a standard design knocked up on a computer, without any care for the personality of the place.

"The planners probably asked when they'd drawn it up: 'Where are we to drop this square?' like the enemy had asked earlier, 'Where are we to drop this bomb?'" he joked.

There isn't the usual concentration of cafés that you find in most town squares. Monday's shuttered up shops weren't helping the atmosphere either. (Don't look around a French town on a Monday if closed shops bother you.) For a minute we stopped in our tracks, wondering whether it was worth staying at all, but Declan couldn't understand our difficulty. "What's the problem with shops not open, when we're not shopping?" he asked with his usual clean-cut logic.

"It's the atmosphere it creates, of course," said Treasa.

It's true that the buzz of buying and selling around you gives off a pulse that shut shops never can.

You get a sense of French people's great love of leisure from their closing times. As well as Monday closing, you've a long midday shutdown. This is a country of sit-down lunches. Business stops for these venerable hours. If you pay for one hour of parking at a meter at noon, the clock speeds around to three in the afternoon. And, as for Sunday closing, that has a special sacredness about it, though not for reasons of religious worship, more in reverence to the god of leisure.

We spotted one open shop, a newsagent, and I went in to buy a book on Abbeville. It took a while to get served. The woman behind the counter and an elderly customer were arguing over which of them should be the more remorseful for some error or other that had been made.

"I'm sorry."

"No, it's I who should be sorry."

"No, it was my fault."

The French have a habit of that. Sometimes when you say thank you, they say, "It's I who should thank you," and you nearly have an argument over which of you should be most grateful.

Goodness knows there's hardly any need to add more conflict than you already have to deal with in this country. France, after all, is the home of contention. Compromise is not their highest priority. It probably has come down the line from the French revolutionaries who gained rights by standing up to authority. Power passed to the people, and the French seem to believe it's their duty to breathe life daily into this spirit of protest. They take to the streets at the slightest whiff of trouble, raise the barricades, block roads and ports. But what's interesting about French protests is that it is a kind of festive hostility. The rest of the population puts up with the inconvenience and newspapers show maps of protest routes. Where else would it happen?

While the two women fought it out over which of them was

most at fault I looked at some books on Abbeville. This small newsagent had a surprisingly broad selection. We wouldn't have done better if the main bookshop had been open.

So we began our self-guided tour of Abbeville with its Gothic showpiece, the church of Saint Vulfran. This was a church about which Victor Hugo once wrote glowingly to his wife and that connection made us all the more eager to visit it. This church was restored after its wartime battering but it looks a little out of place among the modern buildings that surround it. In fact, it was a small miracle that it remained on its feet at all through the aerial bombardment, while the secular buildings fell all around it.

As we approached, a bride in fine brocade was arriving in a blaze of camera flashes. The wedding party was a real show of French style. A few of the men wore gold jackets. Even in secular France the church wedding is *de rigueur*. We stood aside in case some freak photographer should turn his attention to us. Not that that was likely – we would have been a dull addition to such a glittering event, apart from Treasa, who always looks as though she's dressed for the most splendid of occasions. But Steve, in his baggy tracksuit, would have looked like some wanderer who had strayed into the album.

A Gothic structure like Saint Vulfran's is a clear indicator of a prosperous local economy. It was the cloth industry that brought wealth to this area, as early as the eleventh century. They raised sheep on the surrounding fertile hills though not a single sheep was to be seen the day we were there. They washed the wool in the two arms of the river Somme that crosses the town and Abbeville became a great inland port. Boats made their way up to the harbour from far-off lands, until business went downhill and the textile industry crossed the small stretch of channel to England. Jean-Baptiste Colbert – Louis XIV's famous minister – was troubled about French wool making this round trip – leaving the country raw and returning woven, and he tried to rescue Abbeville's cloth in the seventeenth century. But it never regained its original glory. Today, you wouldn't wash much wool in the silted-up river water and there's not much of a sense of harbour either, save for the eleventh-century sailors' chapel. We made a very quick visit to this small church but, apart from reminding you of the town's maritime history, it was disappointing, because the stained glass had been modernized – blandly, I thought.

The closeness to England of this part of northern France encourages crowds to cross *La Manche,* as the channel is called on the French side, on day trips, to stock up their wine supplies and go home in the evening. There's nothing new about this. Even in the early centuries they tripped across the channel at their ease. The short journey meant war was declared at will or at other times peace was declared with a marriage proposal. A daughter – the more beautiful the better – could be swiftly dispatched across this narrow strip of sea, and this worked out a whole lot less expensive than war. The Tudor connection with France – between declarations of war and proposals of marriage – was long-standing. Mary Tudor, sister of Henry VIII, was ferried to nearby Boulogne in 1514 to do her "national service" – marry the ageing King Louis XII of France. Declan calls it the European Union of its time, though, he says the EU, for all its faults, has managed to do a better job in keeping war at bay than the marriages of old.

Mary was assured the dying Louis wouldn't detain her too long and that when her task was complete she could marry whom she liked. (A widow could choose her second husband. One marital sacrifice was enough.) Mary was in love with the splendid Suffolk, a man of low birth, and that must have helped her look to a future beyond her French assignment.

It was to Abbeville she was taken to meet her shook-looking groom and they hosted a ball in the town for her. The dauphin and future King, Francis I, was given the task of escorting her to Abbeville. It was a job he was good at. He loved good-looking women and Mary was that and jolly as well. Her portrait was said to have put Maximilian of Austria into a trance-like state for half an hour. But however captivated Francis might have been that day, his mother, Louise, was not so enthralled. Her worry was that Mary would produce a son and that would knock her own son out of line as heir to the throne.

The groom had regained some of his vigour for the occasion. Just nine months earlier Louis had cried to his dead wife, Anne of Brittany, to make the vault big enough for the two of them. He arrived in Abbeville on a Spanish steed, embraced Mary, offered her jewels one by one and asked for kisses in return. (After his death Mary smuggled a precious diamond he had given her – the Mirror of Naples, a French heirloom – out of the country.)

Mary Tudor was briefly Queen of France. Three months after the marriage the criers were sent through the streets of Paris to announce the King's death. Mary was impounded for six weeks in the Hôtel de Cluny. A child conceived before that time could legally be the heir to the French throne. But none was, and Francis and his mother could breathe easily again.

We didn't find out where the exact assembly point for the meeting of the departing Crusaders was, and when Treasa and I commented on what scant trace of this big event was evident, Declan took us literally.

"What did you expect?" he asked, "that the hills would be streaked in blood?"

Admittedly, it was stretching it somewhat to expect the traces of an eleventh-century event to still be visible. In the imagination it was easy to invent the scene on the hills of Abbeville. The elevated ground would have shown off this cream of Europe's chivalry going on their long trip to fight for their God, bearing the sign of the cross. He was of course from the west, God. He didn't care much for the infidels of the east and that's why they went to rout them from the holy places and rain fire on them, as God, no doubt, would have wished.

Fleeting though our visit was, we were all pleased we'd had a look around. The little crash course in the town's history gave us more of a sense of the place and made us feel our holiday had begun, though it did leave us tight for lunch. Our aim was to eat in the little village of Ducey and then go on to visit nearby Mont Saint-Michel.

# CHAPTER 3

It was exhilarating to be on our way as we took the road by Rouen, Caen and Avranches. Our spirits swept along in the energy of the sun-bathed landscape as it opened out before us, rising, swelling, bending, stretching over the brow of hills, raking in the early-afternoon light. There are parts around here where fields have a fineness about them that compares to velvet, or castor sugar, as if the soil had been sieved. From Rouen it changes to a more robust texture. It is higher, more windswept and woody, no more sieving of soil. Some hills have a topping of green foliage, like the wigs of the gentry of the old regime. The wind doesn't spare its breath around these parts. That frenzied breeze, whose long custom it was to scatter all the energy in its path, is now tamed, captured and converted into electricity through the wind turbines that were whirring in the distant uplands.

The sat nav has done something similar for direction – gathered it from a scatter of maps and guidebooks and funneled it into a single device.

Declan dislikes satellite navigation though Steve had insisted on bringing one on the trip. Declan agreed but it was half-hearted agreement and he kept on ignoring its advice. "I've a sat nav in my head," he explained, when Treasa asked him why he liked irritating it so much.

"You shouldn't be telling it about its rival in your head. You know how jealous technology can be. Give it a bit of love," Steve said.

The first sign for an *aire* (French motorway stop) sent a shiver of delight through me, like the first sighting of swallows in summer. Few countries set up their *aires de l'autoroute* with the same coaxing care as the French. They arrange them tenderly, giving them an ambience that draws you in, to share the local love of eating in the open air, of leisure, of holidays. And the feeling is returned by the great numbers who visit this country.

The word *aire* always rekindles in me my first experience of one. It was somewhere on the road from Paris to Brittany (I've tried several times to locate it but never managed to find the exact spot). A garage with a shop attached shaded from view the picnic area behind it. So it was a surprise to find, at the back of the building, a rustic scene that stirred a yearning to laze for hours. Tables were placed on a hill that rambled upwards towards a wood. A gurgling sound came from a little stream that trickled pristine water where the ground folded between two hillocks. Three men in short-sleeved shirts were eating at a table beneath a tree. They were drawing out the end of their meal with cherries and a bottle of red Burgundy. You might as well have been miles away from the mad multitude on the motorway for all it seeped into this spot. This is a country where eating casts a spell. Put a meal before the French and time stands still. To rush is irreverent.

I asked the men if it was safe to drink the water from a tap that was further in towards the wood. It wasn't, they told me. One of them held out their almost-full bottle of Volvic.

"But I couldn't take it," I said. "*Merci,* but no."

That only made them more insistent and all three became intent on getting me to accept.

"OK, I'll pay for it then," I offered.

They dismissed my offer: *"Non, non, Absolument pas."*

"But I insist," I said, feeling by then somewhat enfeebled against their united force.

They just waved their hands mockingly at my perseverance, as if I had introduced philistine notions of commerce into this blessed spot. When we had eaten and drunk we set off on our way. We had a long drive ahead of us. As we left the men were still there, the picture of leisure, finishing off their wine. They interrupted their chat to give us a wave. Leisure is the word I will always associate with *aire*.

Leisure is something at which the French excel. It conflicts with their stridency, their willingness to take to the streets, raise the barricades and block the ports. But it does tie in with other aspects of life, their attitude towards work, for example. The French show a definite preference for gross national pleasure rather than gross national product. The word for work in French is *travail,* a word associated with toil and hardship in English. France's working week is one of the shortest in the world and they don't believe in working too far into old age either. The employment rate for over-fifty-five-year-olds is lower than average and they protested loudly when retirement age was raised to sixty-two.

When Treasa was making reservations earlier in the year, she had tried to book a hotel for the last week in June. The proprietor told her this was their annual summer holiday – the month of June. Fancy that, the peak season in the tourist business? But here's the interesting thing: she went on to say they had been taking their holidays at the same time for thirty years, since they first went into the hotel business. Maybe the French have it right – work at a leisurely pace and stick with it rather than work all the hours God sends, then collapse into retirement – the slow burner rather than the burnout. Perhaps it's a telling statistic too that the French live longer than the British or the Americans.

As we approached Ducey, Mont Saint-Michel jumped into view. When this mount peeked its spired head over the horizon there was something almost disturbing about the moment. Breathtaking it was, this magic castle in the air, piercing the heavens with mysticism and half-revealed secrets. It was like a spot where angels dwell.

Treasa suggested that we stop and take a look.

"Stop on the motorway?" asked Declan. When it comes to driving, he doesn't credit her with the least knowledge.

"Of course not," she said.

But by the time we came to the next motorway stop, the mount had disappeared – like a mischievous child playing hide and seek – and we had to drive off again, getting into the line of traffic, with all the inconvenience that involved. Steve reminded us that stopping like this would make us late for lunch in Ducey.

We were late anyway. We arrived just minutes after the last lunch was served in Auberge de la Sélune. The waitress checked with the chef to see if anything could be done for us.

Treasa urged us not to give up hope, as if faith might move a mountain or, more miraculous still, make a French chef cook a meal outside the allotted hours. While we waited for the verdict we read the menu through the glass-panelled door – *pie au crabe, noix de Saint-Jacques Provencale* and a list of other temptations – and our hopes beat rapidly. In vain. The waitress came back shaking her head even before she reached us, and we had to leave glumly to try and find somewhere else. Somehow, being an hour late is not half as annoying as missing something by minutes. We had eaten there before. They serve traditional French cuisine: fresh fish from the Sélune River, elaborate pastries, Béarnaise sauce. Ah what's the use in going on? It had been my idea to stop there for lunch, and the others – hungry and tired – I felt sure were trying to find someone to blame. I would have been if I'd been them. I had my argument ready: it wasn't I who had suggested stopping to view Mont Saint-Michel, though, admittedly, I was a willing accomplice. Nothing was said, and so my script didn't have to be pulled out this time. But I felt sure it would stand me in good stead before our holiday ended.

Though Ducey is classified as a *village étape* (a stage town) – just minutes off the A84 motorway (*autoroute des estuaries*) – you cannot just drop by and expect something to eat at any hour of the day. The French respect for closing time was manifesting itself in the noisy roll of shutters. We did finally find a place, Bar de la Baie, where even if the food was not exactly gourmet, they were friendly and patient towards stragglers. The proprietor – well, I think he was the proprietor – cheerfully interrupted his own lunch to prepare a salad for us. And the customers seated at the tables turned their heads around to take a look at us. When I wondered why they were staring, Steve explained:

"It's not every day they come across people speaking French so badly."

"Speak for yourself," said Treasa, who dislikes comments on her standard of French.

"And late for lunch to boot," said Declan

Ducey has sure grown sophisticated. In the space of a decade or so I've seen it grow from a lifeless rural village to a proper little beauty, a *ville fleurie*. Ville fleurie status means window boxes, flower pots and hanging baskets, gushing and pouring from every window sill; roundabouts and parks covered in a veritable artwork of floral symmetry, releasing every scent known to man or insect.

After lunch we went to the *boulangerie-pâtisserie* for a takeaway dessert. On the window there were cakes with names that call to mind images of France's proud tradition of pastry making – *Paris-Brest, tarte aux pommes, religieuse* (a name that used to confuse me until I looked more carefully at its form. It's a cream éclair in the shape of a nun). I'm sure it's no accident that the words *pâtisserie* (confectionery) and *tapisserie* (tapestry) are so close, because the craft in both compares well. We chose a *flan nature,* a *religieuse*, and two *Paris-Brest*. A woman in pink wrapped them lovingly. They were going to enjoy their florid packaging for such a short time that I was going to suggest not to bother but I was glad I let her finish. She shaped the colourful paper into little pyramids, making them look worthy of gifts that were about to undergo the most solemn of presentations. We ate them near the fountain in the little park beside the seventeenth-century Montgomery castle. Biting into one of these works of craft seemed shameful but you quickly got over it in this country where few rituals are as sacred as eating.

Montgomery castle is more like a big house than a castle. It is now used for exhibitions and community events. An ancestor of the Montgomery family, Gabriel I, has the uncomfortable distinction of being the person who accidentally killed King Henry II. While the

King was taking part in a tournament, a splinter from a lance went into his eye and lodged in his brain.

It is unfortunate to kill anyone accidentally, but to kill a king must have been especially embarrassing. The country went through a lot of hardship as a result of his death. It brought an end to strong monarchy. Henry had been good at playing off his powerful enemies – the Guise of Loraine and the Bourbon – against one another. His widow, Catherine de Medici (of the great Florentine family) took over as regent and she had the double drawback of being a woman and a foreigner. In crises she had a habit of losing her head, not literally of course (I thought I'd better clarify that in the country that invented the guillotine). Before her husband took his last breath on 10 July 1559, he prayed that his people would remain faithful to the Catholic faith. Steve said it was mighty decent of him to think of his countrymen and their devotion at a moment when most people would have been thinking of themselves. France remained Catholic all right, but at a high cost. His death was followed by a thirty-five-year-long civil war between Catholics and Protestants, each side trying to outdo one another in carnage.

Declan was keen not to delay in Ducey but Treasa and I wanted to take a stroll by the river. Steve came up with a half-way solution, a short walk. He's good at pooling likes and dislikes and he has the knack of coming up with a blend that leaves everyone happy. That's the benefit of a group – desires get diluted, divided out and blended, and you don't get a chance to soak excessively in your own essence. Because, may God spare us from what we want. And if he won't, someone else must step in, like the others in the group, who are not getting what they want either. Mix and match, give and take and you end up with a tapestry – the good form of one, the highs of another, the rants and sulks of someone else and so on and so on and so on. The after-lunch amble by the Sélune was relaxing. We could hear the waters gurgling like ghostly beings whispering and boasting about their exploits of the night before. It was relaxing and it allowed us to digest our meal with ease, French-style. Already we had taken on some of the local habits.

# CHAPTER 4

When we reached Avranches it rang out with the chimes of multiple bells like a musical accompaniment as we walked around the town. In the heyday of pilgrimage this was the final stopping point for those on their way to Mont Saint-Michel. No two bells called out the hour in unison and it sounded like a dispute in poor time keeping. Of course if they had agreed on the time, few would notice their great number. But whatever their point was, it would be seriously inadvisable to set your watch by any of them.

The large number of French churches and religious sites date from a time when the Church got tipsy on its own power and cloaked it in architectural piety. The clergy got the idea they would seduce their flock with a building spree. And they did, until their flock wanted to be seduced no more, not with churches anyway.

French schools swung from veritable theological seminaries to centres of anti-clericalism. So says Marcel Pagnol, one of France's great writers. After the Revolution, when the French were swept off their feet with the ideas of liberty, equality and fraternity, the Republicans took to the pulpit and put education to work on a new dogma. The Church, they said, had hoodwinked the people with fables of damnation and salvation. But the new doctrine of Republicanism would expose all their scheming.

Anti-clerical fever heated up after the shameful Prussian defeat of France in 1870, ending with the legal separation of church and state in 1905. This stridency finally cooled off in the trenches of World War I, in the brotherhood of combat, not quite the big-hearted fraternity French revolutionaries had in mind.

Steve thinks the French take lay fervour a little too far, that their inflexible secularism ends up replacing one dogma with another. "But the French are happy with their arrangement and why should I worry about it," he said.

They're very happy with it indeed. Still, they're ever so proud of their religious sites. They have even been called symbols of national unity by the very people who consider secularism their greatest policy.

The thing was the French backlash at religion, angry and all as it was, never got so vexed as to strip off church roofs and melt down bells. That is a great blessing for today's tourist. Holidaymakers come in their droves to gaze at these great feats of structure, to feast their eyes on colourful stained glass and to soak in the antiquity of it all.

The great church-building zeal hit medieval Europe between the middle of the eleventh and the mid-fourteenth century when eighty cathedrals, five hundred large churches and several thousand small churches were built in France alone. A building binge like this would never happen again. It was as costly as the big railway projects of the nineteenth century or the price of a war. Indeed war and religious architecture fed off one another in the Middle Ages in that a lot of technical tricks learned from war were applied to church building. Treasa says you can still see the link between the two, that the spires look warlike, like arrows pointing at the heavens.

Village churches are now hugely out of proportion to the needs of their thin populations, even if they were interested in worship. And interested they are not. Out of the eighty per cent of French people who are baptised, only ten per cent go to church. I haven't seen statistics on how many believe in God, how many take the advice of their much respected philosopher, Blaise Pascal, who thought you might as well believe in God because if he didn't exist, you would lose nothing, whereas if he did, believing in him might earn you a place in heaven.

We made a quick visit to the church of Saint Gervais and dropped into the museum – the scriptorial – that houses in darkness the illuminated manuscripts that were rescued from the scriptorium of Mont Saint-Michel Abbey at the time of the French Revolution. The ancient scripts glowed like lanterns. They cannot be allowed look broad daylight in the eye in case it would fade their ancient colours. It took a few minutes to find our bearings as we moved from bright to dark. Our short visit didn't do them justice at all. We were in a hurry to tie in with tidal times because we wanted to approach the Abbey of Mont Saint-Michel, which is built on an island rock on the mouth of the Couesnon River, by the causeway.

This is the loveliest of approaches to the abbey. Ever since I had seen pictures of hikers – ruck-sacked, high-booted and carefree – doing this trek across to the mount I had been planning to go this way.

The longest walk – starting from west of Avranches – is thirteen kilometres and it takes over five hours. That is a long time to walk that distance. It's the resistance of the sand against your feet that slows you down. There are shorter routes, which the not-so-fit can take.

"Perhaps you'd be interested in this walk," suggested the woman in the tourist office, whose glasses looked fixed to the crown of her head. She ran her pen over the finely detailed map, pointing out the shortest route across the inlet. I followed the movement of her biro. You could have thrown something across the tiny opening (a rucksack perhaps. It would save you the trouble of carrying it). Was that as much as we looked able for, I wondered?

Steve, it seems, was thinking the same. He turned to us and said with a laugh: "That wouldn't be a feat worth bothering with. It would hardly earn a line in a message back home. And what's the point in doing something impressive unless there's someone to impress?"

She must have heard him. She said, as if to frighten us, "It's two kilometres."

And she still wasn't done with dampening our spirits. "The ground is soft, you know."

I could feel my enthusiasm ebbing away. And just at that

moment, as if to save our pride, the window lit up in a flash of lightening.

"That decides it. We're not going to cross the bay in a storm," said Steve.

And so ended my long-hatched plan. It turned out to be a lot more hardship than those light-hearted pictures conveyed. And we went, like the other million tourists who visit this site each year, across the timber footbridge.

# CHAPTER 5

We took a moment to look at Mont Saint-Michel before crossing the bridge. It was an instant you wanted to devour, to feel its feelings, to get into the rustling layers of its history. The spire-topped mount rose, jagged-edged, throwing its triangular reflection into the water, showing off all the thought that went into its construction. This once was a hive of learning, preservation and piety. A community of monks clung like bees to a flower, gripping the side of a rock, as if space was the scarcest of commodities in this wide-open countryside.

How they coaxed and humoured buildings into being back then, how they infused them with the life of the universe, not just to fit in with the tides but with the constellations too, the undercurrents, the wind, the seasons, the pulse of the rock. It looks as if all of nature was consulted before a single stone was laid, so that the mystical could mesh with the liturgical, Christian theology with pagan rites. This perfect harmony was part of the old-world view of things, when out-flowing and inflowing tides were believed to have come from one and the same cosmic breath. That was before science came along and sorted things neatly into separate parcels, split spirit from matter, animate from inanimate.

You can imagine how it spoke to the spirits of the pilgrims long ago as they reached their journey's end. They came here in their droves on 16 October, the feast of Saint Michael the Archangel, returning at the back end of each year, like the melody of the rhyming ends of poetry. They still come here in great numbers though to satisfy other needs now. In the great heyday of pilgrimage, the focus was on denouncing the world and celebrating God. Nowadays it's about taking God to task and celebrating the world. It was easy to condemn a world that gave you a choice between famine or war, salvation or damnation and so anything that seemed as if it could act as a go-between was worth looking into: a mount, a well, a relic or whatever would lessen the pain of existence.

Today, the world is much harder to condemn, what with being able to take a few holidays a year, do your shopping at any hour of the day or night, ring your far-distant friends from the loneliest island, have Google at your fingertips. No one would be unsporting enough to denounce today's world. And so the crowds no longer come here to lessen the pain but to increase the joy. And they tread the ancient stone steps and feast their eyes on the great building skills of their forebears, Romanesque piled in with Gothic and perched on a rock. It is enough to make you feel you have drunk the wine.

"It mightn't have been done with the humblest of intentions but I'm glad they did it," said Treasa, as we walked across the footbridge and joined the long stream of humanity that passed by the entrance. Shops, restaurants, cafés, ice-cream vendors, souvenir stores tempted us with food and drink, sweets and chocolates wrapped in Mont Saint-Michel inscriptions, snow globes and every conceivable item that could be transformed into a souvenir of the visit. Mère Poulard's restaurant is still hail and hearty a century and a half on, still (they claim) serving the great thick omelettes for which she was famous. There's even a hotel or two here where you can spend the night. It looked an enticing thing to do, though your space would be cramped.

The lower level of the rock is the commercial centre. It gets more spiritual as you go upwards. A church on a hilltop dedicated to Saint Michael is not unusual. Places in his honour were perched on heights and churches devoted to him appeared on hilltops all over Europe around the year 1000. He was the archangel, head of the heavenly militia and conqueror of Satan. He was much loved in the era of crusaders and invaders, so they gave him a military look.

His job was to lead the dead and put their souls on the balance on the Day of Judgment. In the Book of Revelation he fights a dragon and wins. Steve said that last piece of information hardly needs saying. "It would be fairly meaningless to tell us about it if the dragon had devoured him. We could accomplish that much ourselves."

Our guide was not modest. He told us several times during the tour how good he was. I thought that might have been for us to judge, but apparently not. He made jokes that unsettled you rather than made you laugh. Treasa wasn't enjoying his wit, which was sometimes directed at her. Even Steve was put to the edge of his patience.

"Maybe his purpose was to put us through a bit of hardship, like the pilgrims of old," said Declan. "After all, we arrived in cars, not on foot like our suffering forbears and that was enough luxury without expecting a pleasant tour as well."

It was a relief when it came to an end.

Mont Saint-Michel dates from the time when Western Europe still had her hobnail boots on. It was altogether inferior in refinement and learning to the Greek east or the Muslim world. Saint Michael's heyday coincided with the time during which the Normans were at the peak of their power. Virile and warlike and all as the Normans were, they came up with some interesting refinements. Until close to the end of the twelfth century they were leaders not just in war but in architecture too. They were ahead of their time in that they were using some designs in church-building that would be later linked with the Gothic period, like the pointed arch. The buildings on Mont Saint-Michel moved in step with the glory of Norman dukes. What began as a simple house of worship at the top of Mont Tombe (as it was originally called) ended in a spectacle that became the marvel of the West.

When the Duke of Normandy invited the Benedictine monks onto the mount in the tenth century he was just being trendy. They were like the spiritual rock stars of their time. The order was so influential from the sixth to the twelfth century that it's often called the

Benedictine Age. The Benedictine Rule called for poverty, obedience and chastity. Their discipline and ritual created a kind of heaven on earth and so to sponsor a monastery was the ambition of every duke. The duke chose the abbot and had a big say in the architecture.

Saint Benedict had said, "My vow of poverty has given me a hundred thousand crowns a year. My vow of obedience has raised me to the rank of sovereign prince." Mont Saint-Michel became the most famous shrine in Northern Europe. Everyone from kings to humble folk came here, so the alms built up highly and splendidly. Looking at it today, with two three-storey buildings balanced on a steep rock, you get a feeling that Benedict's successors might not have remained content with the hundred thousand crowns in figurative form.

After our tour with the greatest tour guide in the world, we came down the steps that wound like a corkscrew around the rock. We stopped at the crypt in the belly of the rock. This small chapel I think is the nicest part of the abbey. Long candles were burning and they bent like drunks in the heat of their own flames. I felt an urge to light one. Mine began to curve nearly instantly. Treasa lit one and it stayed upright. It held its drink better than mine. We knelt on the kneelers. It was nice to add your prayers to the long line that came before you. It made you feel that you had played your small part in the continuity of ritual.

We wound our way around the gardens, which looked ever so like the Garden of Eden – or at least what I think it might have looked like – even down to the apple trees growing on the sloping ground. You could have picked one off a tree, though it would have looked a mighty mean thing to do, and besides if Eve's example is anything to go by, who knows what would befall the universe if you did. Steve thought they were put there to put visitors' resistance to the test. God's immediate vengeance would probably have been a bellyache because it was late June, not yet the season for eating apples in these northern climes. The monks produced their own food, though the apple trees didn't look as if they dated from the tenth century.

We visited the chapel dedicated to Saint Aubert, the Bishop of Avranches. This was the man who began it all. It was he who in his sleep, in the year 708, had a vision from Saint Michael instructing him to build a church in his honour on the mount. Evidently Saint Michael was no slouch when it came to giving orders because he left a finger hole in Aubert's head. We had seen the proof for ourselves earlier, in the treasury (*le trésor*) of the church of Saint Gervais in Avranches. The skull of Aubert was there with a hole the size of a finger. He was in the company of other saints who looked equally capable of impressive stunts. One of these, Saint Denis, patron of France, was holding his severed head in his hands. The story goes that Saint Denis, the first Bishop of Paris, was martyred on the city's highest hill, Montmartre. He picked up his head, as you would, and walked the six miles from Montmartre to the site of where the Basilica of Saint Denis now stands. Steve said that between one with a hole in his head and the other with his head in his hands, times certainly have become a whole lot more staid nowadays.

We went once again to the top of the mount to have another look around before we left. From this height you can take in great eyefuls of Normandy and Brittany. We tried to locate Saint-Pair across the water. It is near Granville and probably too far away to see. What caught our interest in this place was a poem written by a young monk who described the big pilgrimage to Mont Saint-Michel sometime between the years 1154 and 1186, as he looked from his monastery across the bay. He captured in verse the moment of arrival long ago, probably for the great feast of Saint Michael, on 16 October and he makes it feel as if everyone who could have been there that day was, and anyone who couldn't be there would have longed to be. He described the crowd, young and old, singing and reciting lays; minstrels entertaining the crowds with ballads; the cries of the vendors who tried to tempt the pilgrims with some sustenance; the neighing and the whinnying of the chargers, saddle-horses and pack-horses; the sounds of horns, flutes and trumpets. It all seemed like a bit of an outing as well as a holy event.

That day as we looked towards the east a patchwork of fields spread in the distance like a great stretch of beauty going all the way to the horizon. These lands were once part of the vast property of the monks (one of Benedict's rules was that the monasteries should be self-supporting). The fields exhaled a breath of midsummer abundance with their crops of green and gold, ridges of black and corduroy-like streaks of tillage. Lines of trees and hedgerows dotted the landscape. About fifteen kilometres away we could see the rocky hillock of Mont Dol, the mythical abode of Saint Michael before he took his great leap from Mont Dol to Monte Tombe (or Mont Saint-Michel as the world now knows it). The mark of the giant footprint remains there, so they say, though we can offer no proof because we were too far away to see such detail.

Out to sea was the archipelago of the Îles Chausey. That is where most of the abbey's granite came from, hauled across the causeway without footbridge or help. And few worried about the resistance of the sand against their steps in the harsh world of that time, though we showed no gratitude when that consideration was offered to us in the tourist office in Avranches.

It was nice to look at what the medieval monks saw. Or maybe they had little time for idle gazing, what with farming, illuminating manuscripts or losing themselves in prayer and work, the two guiding principles of their order.

Cattle were grazing in the fields. A westerly breeze was blowing, a wind that has carried Atlantic moisture inland since time immemorial. It has charmed the crops with its mist, coaxing them into yielding more and more. And that day it was easy to imagine the same breeze once carrying the sound of the male-voiced chants of the monks to the pastures. It must have been a lovely melody – ritual bells mingling with the lowing of cattle, sounds of matins and other liturgy marking the canonical hours, feasts and seasons, lunar calendars, penitential Lent, Advent, Septuagesima, Quinquagesima alongside their secular cousins, cosmology, alchemy and the signs of the zodiac.

It was time to snap out of our reverie. We came down the steps in single file to allow room for the crowds coming in the opposite direction. Declan said he felt so jolted around by the layers of time that he'd have to go for coffee to find his bearings. And minutes later we settled into the cramped little café at the lower level of the rock.

We all agreed it had been a nice journey into the past. We weren't yet finished with that era. The following day we planned to go to see the cathedral in Chartres, the best-preserved example of Gothic in Europe.

# CHAPTER 6

The way to Chartres from Mont Saint-Michel as the crow flies or as the pilgrim most likely walked is through Domfront, Alençon, Dreux to Chartres. If you travel by motorway you take the road through Rennes, then the A11 highway towards Paris, by Laval and Le Mans. It's longer but faster. Treasa objected to going this way. She said she would like to see what the pilgrims saw, "At least, more or less what they saw."

That amused Steve and Declan and they started pointing out new buildings and saying what a lovely sight they must have been for the pilgrims in the Middle Ages.

"They could have cooled off in the air conditioning of that hotel over there or had a swim in the pool," joked Declan, as he pointed to one of the many hotels near Mont Saint-Michel.

"Of course I don't mean it literally," Treasa said. "I was thinking of the general contours of the horizon. And, you know, they're probably not that different. But the thing is, speed has gone from being the least valued to the most valued in this mad rush to gain time. Once a motorway is on offer it demands some sort of rare courage to take the slow route. And speed misses the very thing that draws you on holidays in the first place," she said.

"Yes, it might," agreed Declan, "but you're right about it needing courage to set off for Chartres on that little road you're suggesting. What time do you think we'd get there?" he asked, pointing out the minor line on the map that she was proposing. "It's all very well seeing what the pilgrims saw, but there are limits."

"I thought holidays were for getting away from timetables and destinations. You might as well be in any country if you travel by motorway. I like roads that wind and meander, not cut through a scene," she said.

"I think it's reasonable to talk about destinations, even on holidays," said Declan.

In the end he agreed, grumpily, to do what she wanted, after having been called an arrivalist. "OK, OK, let's go the slow and difficult way, then. Who wants to arrive anyway? We've only booked into a hotel, but rather than being arrivalists, we can sleep in the car."

I was glad Treasa won the dispute. The hardship of the winding road was more than compensated for by the immediacy of the view. Yellow heads of sunflowers along the way swayed like dancers in the breeze. Approaching hills puffed into rounds like the dough of unbaked bread, the yeast of the fermenting forces of time. Grey-roofed villages appeared over the brow of hills. Poplars with military bearing lined avenues, straight as colonels, chin in, chest out. You could see the deep-blue outline of the horizon where the trees stepped out of the way, so perfect it could have been drawn with a ruler. There was not a defect in sight. Lovely and all as it was, though, it did rather go on and on. I was wondering how Declan was taking it.

Treasa didn't seem to notice. She broke the silence: "I love to follow the changing landscape from start to finish."

"Well at least we've plenty of time to enjoy it," said Declan with a mischievous smile. How many hours have we been travelling now? And we haven't got anywhere yet."

"We should stop at the next *aire*. I'd love a cold drink," she said.

"And where do you think you'll get an *aire* on a road like this, much less a cold drink?"

"OK, OK, let's do without it, so," she said.

In the end Steve came up with a compromise, that we take the motorway for the second half of the journey, and that eased the tension. We arrived in Chartres eventually. Declan compromised too, by using the sat nav to locate our hotel.

31

The following morning we were waiting for them to open the great doors of Chartres Cathedral. We had got up early to prolong the busy day ahead and here we were halted outside closed doors. Steve said it was inconsiderate of them not to have opened them especially early for us, seeing as we'd made such a brave effort to get out of bed. After what seemed like an eternity, they opened the doors, heavily and loftily. It was like opening a cave of treasure.

They can write and talk all they like about Chartres Cathedral's high-flying feats of Gothic – the rib vaults, the gravity, the fenestration – but what caught my delight that morning was the peace of the youthful day, the blue hues of semi-darkness, the sound of our footsteps on the original medieval floor. For the first hour or so we had the place almost to ourselves. A handful of people in the centre of the nave were walking the circles of the labyrinth, some in bare feet. They had come early to perform their ritual while there was still space on the stone maze. Their footwork was hard to follow. They stepped forward, then backward, then forward again. They seemed to be trying to get as many steps as possible out of the limited space on the labyrinth, along the loops towards the centre. If the labyrinth were stretched out in a straight line the journey would be twenty-six metres in length.

Treasa wanted to find out how she could try this ritual, or whatever it was. She enquired but no one could help her and they shrugged accordingly. Or maybe they did know but an explanation was too complex to get through the fog of different languages.

The labyrinth idea came from ancient Greece, from Daedalus, who created the original labyrinth on Crete. No one could find their way through the maze. Theseus, slayer of the Minotaur, found the path only with the help of Ariadne's thread. For Christianity, it was God's grace that was the guide. By stepping it out on the ringed path – the road to Jerusalem – moving from the outside inwards, pilgrims short-cut the route to heaven. It symbolised, as far as anyone can tell, that the wisest route through life is inwards, to the spiritual centre of being. And, like life, it's a path full of knots, tangles and rows (as our argument about how best to travel to Chartres had shown). Pagan and Christian preached the same message, that we cannot find our way through without help.

The labyrinth in Chartres dates from around 1200. It is the largest and best that survives from the period. The battle between Theseus and the Minotaur was once engraved on the copper plaque in the centre, but in 1792 the copper found more useful things to do than point the way to the inner being. It was melted down along with the cathedral bells to make cannons for Napoleon's wars. Now only the metal studs remain.

Treasa and I went to see the windows. They cover about an acre of wall. Declan said he would explore the outside. Steve wasn't on for poring over windows either. Their disinterest led Treasa to conclude they were both colour blind.

"I'm not colour blind. It's just I'm not interested," said Declan touchily.

But she was insistent. "A lot of men are. They say men are dogs and women are cats."

At this piece of information the three of us stood looking at her waiting for further clarification.

"What might that mean?" enquired Declan at last.

"Dogs can only see in black and white," she explained.

Steve burst into a laugh that echoed around the cathedral.

"And who in the name of goodness knows what colour dogs can see?" asked Declan.

"They carried out a survey," said Steve. "A thousand dogs were interviewed."

I enjoyed the trade windows most. They have a matter-of-factness about them, a record of solid work compared to the lofty windows of the Virgin Mary, the apostles or luminaries like Charlemagne. In a way, they show what the age was capable of. The twelfth century – when the cathedral was built – was a time of sprouting confidence, when towns began to prosper and cathedral schools started to thrive. These new centres of learning celebrated the world, unlike their predecessors, the monastic schools, where teaching was intent on denouncing the world. Chartres was a leading cathedral school, which took its knowledge from all sources. And the cathedral shows traces of this global guidance: Arab mathematics, ritual, geomancy, astrology, alchemy, Greek elemental forces of creation and destruction. They are all represented, challenging heaven with seductive curves.

The trade windows are at a lower level, which is logical enough, to have them at less heavenly heights, but it also made commercial sense to locate them in the best advertising position. There are windows to tailors, furriers, carpenters, coopers, stoneworkers, shoemakers, butchers, wine merchants, water carriers, bakers. Treasa said that whoever thought mass marketing was invented in modern times didn't know the Middle Ages.

"Nothing changes really," said Declan, who had joined us in having a look at the windows, despite his "colour blindness". "Only instead of building cathedrals we're building shopping malls and sports arena now. They're our cathedrals, but I doubt if anyone will be visiting them ten centuries from now."

The only way we could drag Treasa away from the cathedral was by suggesting we could have another look the following day. Steve wanted to drive by Beauce, the great plateau south of Paris, to the east of Chartres. Treasa wondered why, because she had read that it was the most boring place on earth – vast plains of corn, corn and more corn.

"Just to see how bored I can get," he quipped. When he told us that it was the setting of Victor Hugo's poem "Le Semeur" ("The Sower") and for Millet's paintings: Le Semeur and L'Angelus, our interest lit up.

I didn't find Beauce boring at all. It looked like a great sea of sustenance, swaying and curving in the golden breeze. Wheat-growing here must have produced sheaves of money over the centuries when you think of the great part bread has played in French civilization. (A book has been written on the subject, Le Pain Maudit (Cursed Bread), by American historian Steven L. Kaplan.) This land was part of the wealth of the Diocese of Chartres, thirty-five square kilometres of it. In due course the produce of these fields

34

would show itself off in the Gothic spires and jewel-like windows of the cathedral. As well as corn, this land produced wool. If you add tithes and dues to all of that you get a fair clatter of cash. Beauce supplied most of the limestone for the cathedral too. For hundreds of years after the fall of Rome they no longer used stone in buildings. But from the tenth century on, when it came back in fashion, they couldn't get enough stone and they raked the countryside in search of it.

I can't remember whose idea it was to leave Chartres that evening and have dinner in Voves, but it sounded good, so we headed for Hôtel Le Quai Fleuri, about twenty kilometres or so from Chartres. Voves was charmingly hard to find. We had to comb our way through secret countryside, on a spiderweb of roads where you would be quite likely to find a cat sleeping in the car's way. Crossroads, junctions without signs, narrow twists and turns, a railway bridge and other complications added to the remote evening charm. We had the place to ourselves, which was just as well because even on these slender roads locals have a habit of clipping along as if they are on a racing track. Hardly a movement disturbed the peace except for the whistles and chirps of the birds.

We were all set to eat on the terrace but we had to move indoors because the insects were bothering us. They had especially turned their attention to Steve. He's like a magnet for flying creatures. Bees, flies, mosquitoes, whatever – they cannot resist him. Bats have flown into him. Once he swallowed a bee and another time a seagull pooed on his head. It was that last piece of information that made us speedily move indoors. There was no shortage of tables. It was still quite early; we're always first into French restaurants. French people tend to eat a little later and our appetites hadn't yet made the adjustment for local time. After an hour or so other clients began to file in and soon every table was full.

Treasa is never as happy as when she's surveying a menu. This is truly her country, the place where she feels most at home because here everyone is a bit like her when it comes to food. She talks dreamily about the most ordinary culinary things – the perfect flip of a pancake (which, now that we were in France, was a crêpe), the exact moment when a melon is ripe, the precise instant when a soufflé is ready. In a way her words fall on deaf ears because the three of us are not such fine-tuned foodies as to care if a soufflé is left in the oven an instant after the instant of perfection. But in another way they don't because to listen to someone so committed has a certain power of transference, even on to people as resistant as us.

Not only does Treasa get excited about what she's going to choose, she wants to know what everyone else is going to order too.

"What are you having?" she asked us, going from one to the other with the eagerness of a child in Toyland.

In French restaurants they take the whole order together: starter, main course and dessert. It's something I find hard to get used to because it's not easy to predict what kind of dessert you might like before you even begin. Treasa suggests various options and combinations. Often when you don't take her advice you end up sorry you didn't. She'll say things like: "They don't go well together. You'd be better off with a lighter dessert because you'll feel too full after such a heavy main course." Or sometimes she'll amaze you by saying something like: "You ordered that dessert that time we were in London and you found it too sweet."

We gaze at her in wonder.

"But that was nearly six years ago. How do you remember?"

Declan finds it all a bit too probing, too detective-like and it nearly puts him off his meal. That evening in Voves he said, "Which of these desserts would I like to have this evening Treasa? Have I ordered this in the last ten years, by any chance?"

She got cross with him: "I'm just being penalised for having a good memory."

Declan is the expert on wine. Not that he holds the menu with the same caress as Treasa, but he does soften. That's the thing about people when they're doing something they love, they nearly take on its shape. Boundaries melt like wax in the warmth between lover and loved.

We lingered delightfully over dinner. We chatted idly about

everything and anything – the ideal holiday, the ideal menu, the ideal place to live, the ideal person to live with, the ideal… then someone noticed that night was falling. We grabbed the bill. Steve speedily keyed in his pin on the credit card machine and we scurried out of the place as if it was on fire, paying no attention to the polite waiter who thanked us for our custom and bade us goodbye. People were looking at us wondering why we were leaving with such a sense of purpose. We had the labyrinth of roads back to Chartres to negotiate.

Declan was still at the table busily calculating the best route home. He had "forgotten" the sat nav. We all knew about his little absent-mindedness and if ever there was an occasion to complain, this was one. But why would we want to deprive him of his holiday's greatest pleasure? If ever they invented a device to navigate the way around a menu, I bet Treasa would be the first to grumble. And to give her credit, she didn't say a cross word to him that evening.

Next morning we went to Combray, Marcel Proust's fictitious Illiers. The village is so linked with his fiction that it is now called Illiers-Combray. It was the home of Elisabeth Amiot, the Tante Léonie (Aunt Léonie) of his writing. She was his father's sister and Proust and his family spent holidays there when he was a child. The trip by train is told in haunting detail – leaving the station, the journey from Paris, changing trains at Chartres for the final leg of the journey to Illiers. These holidays were the inspiration for his writings. The house is a museum now, preserved even down to the bottle of Vichy water, placed at the bedside, with which the bedridden Tante Léonie took her medicine. Across the corridor, in a smaller bedroom, is the young Marcel's magic lantern which he made so famous.

The hall door opens straight on to Rue du Docteur Proust, named after Marcel's father. A few hundred metres down the road are the gardens designed by his aunt's husband, where the family took walks and had picnics by the Vivonne River. This was Proust's fictional Parc de Swann and his words still linger in the place.

What struck me most was the smallness of the house, how

ordinary it was, the limited size of the pavement below Tante Léonie's window, the theatre of her expansive gossip. Then there was the little kitchen where Francoise, the family maid, prepared the meals. Where did everyone fit? It didn't feel big enough to contain all the memories that tumbled so sensuously from Proust's pen. And that's its secret I suppose, because more than anything else, it shows the expansive eyes of childhood. There before you is the magic such an ordinary setting can inspire, the memories it has left to generations of readers.

"Ah childhood, those are the days," said Treasa, putting into words what I was thinking. "To make us grow up from that state of wonder must surely be God's retribution on us. Never mind what we were told about God turning his vengeance on us over Eve eating that stupid little apple. Or if he did, it better have tasted good."

We just managed a brief visit to the church that Proust painted so vividly in his writing, before it closed. The woman dangled the door keys noisily from her hand as she waited, which I thought was a gesture of her intent to get us out quickly so she could lock up. But I might have been wrong; she took a long time to show us the pew on the left-hand side where the Amiot family used to sit.

Next morning we were ready to leave Chartres, except for one last thing we had to see, the *camisa,* the cathedral's prized possession. It's a tunic, said to have been worn by Mary, some say during the birth of Christ, others say at the time of the Annunciation. Declan reckons since both are equally untrue it hardly matters. It performed all sorts of miracles. And, in turn, it was saved by a miracle. When the Romanesque church and much of the town of Chartres were destroyed in a great fire on 10 June 1194, the *camisa* was rescued by two gallant priests who rushed into the burning building, hair-raisingly dodging the rain of burning cinders and melting lead. The *camisa* is now held in a reliquary in the northeast chapel of the apse. Alas, it was closed that day because they were doing some restoration work.

"What a shame," Treasa said.

But Declan thought when you see what it looked like from an image, what did it matter?

Treasa thought this rather missed the point. "Shouldn't we have stayed at home altogether in that case," she said, "and looked at images of France instead."

"But you don't want perpetuating all that fiction," said Declan.

I think Treasa and Declan like testing their opposing views on each other. They enjoy the reassuring balance they find in their differences, like teenagers airing their rebellious opinions in the comfort of knowing that their parents are at hand to step in and save them from their own excesses.

The following morning we were ready to leave Chartres and be on our way for our next destination, the little village of Quarré-les-Tombes in Burgundy, or, more precisely, in Morvan.

# CHAPTER 7

It was Treasa who convinced us to divert to the Morvan region. She admitted afterwards that the pull of a nice hotel near Quarré-les-Tombes had a hand in her decision. Sometimes you get exaggerated accounts of hotels on internet sites and brochures, but not in the case of Auberge de l'Atre. They say they think of every detail for the enjoyment of their guests. That is true. Yet when you're there, it is all done so smoothly that you imagine it just falls into place without any effort behind it.

The only downside was Treasa's reaction to an English teacher who was staying there and who was intent on helping her with every word of French she uttered. It's a bit irksome when you're struggling with a language to be overheard by another anglophone who can speak French a whole lot better than you. It's worse when they won't let a single thing go without passing comment on it. When Treasa asked the white-starched waiter who was taking our order what the word *estragon* meant, a voice rang out across the dining-room floor from about two tables away: "Tarragon." The next translation was for *bar*. It means, the explanation came, bass. More interpreting followed.

The teacher must have had great hearing, because Treasa was keeping her voice low. A few people were looking around to catch a glimpse of the people behind the voices of this linguistic exchange. As the waiter passed her table, she said to him, "We teachers never finish our work you know."

"That's just too bad for the rest of us," said Treasa under her breath.

It was making us all uptight. Steve said the best solution was to text one another to make sure the rest of our conversation wasn't translated.

"She probably means well," said Declan.

But Treasa was in no mood for concessions. "Well she can be well-meaning somewhere else."

"The thing is if we look at ourselves, we might be carrying every bit as much job freight as she is, without knowing it," said Declan. "Because it's no easy task to unform yourself from the shape your work has moulded you into the minute you're on holidays."

Breakfast next morning was cosy and colourful. Floral cups and tall coffee jugs glowed against the dark wood of a large communal table. The closeness to the other guests put our language skills to the test. Language is not just about words. You have to get around how people interact in a different culture. How do you begin a casual chat? Every culture has its own starter. Treasa enquired about the best places to visit around the area and that worked well in getting the talk flowing. The teacher wasn't there so we could make even more mistakes than usual. Over crunchy baguette, warm croissants and steaming pots of coffee we swapped ideas on where best to spend the day. There was a couple there from Dijon and they said Abbaye de Fontenay, Avallon and Noyers-sur-Serein were worth seeing.

Everything was going wonderfully well until the teacher appeared. She addressed us all chirpily, in perfect French. Isn't there something about people who are bubbly in the early morning that's a little trying? It's not fair at all that someone's good humour should put you in a bad mood but somehow it can. She had a special word for Treasa. She had been listening to her the evening before (well we knew that) and she told her she had "done rather well at making herself understood." This made it sound like she had been using sign language, when, in truth, Treasa quite fancies herself as a French speaker. Treasa just answered frostily: "Thank you." The teacher's husband was a silent man. I would say he could have told her a thousand times to confine her teaching to the classroom. In vain.

In the low morning sun that Sunday, we drove from Quarré-les-Tombes, through a web of D roads, crossing the A6 motorway, the *autoroute du soleil,* by pastoral countryside, on our way to the Abbey of Fontenay, France's oldest surviving Cistercian foundation. The beige of its chalky stone walls glowed in the sun's rays. A black-suited woman led a tour around the buildings, which were set around a courtyard, and she told us in French, which was spoken as if she was trying to fit as many words into the shortest possible space of time, that it was Bernard of Clairvaux who had founded the place. Sparseness was Cistercian policy – to shed the worldly ornamentation of monasteries – and sparseness in joy was Bernard's belief too because he thought you should shed all fun if you wanted to get to heaven. His rise was rapid; he became the central figure of the order. By the mid twelfth century there were nearly four hundred Cistercian monasteries in Europe and a Cistercian Pope in Rome. Bernard clashed intensely with the eager spirit of enquiry that was part of the Gothic age – classical learning, philosophy, law, analysing God, those sort of things.

We all found the visit a quieting experience. Steve said the place had a tranquility about it. "It's good for the soul," he said and this uncharacteristic outburst made Declan take a second glance at him. Steve must have noticed because he went on to explain his unusual comment. "When you're self employed, between trying to keep your customers happy, steal business from your rivals and look for payment for the work you've done, you go through a certain amount of spiritual leakage," he said. And then, as if half embarrassed by his lofty words, he nudged Treasa and said, "That's how you'd put it, isn't it? It's contagious, all this spiritual chat."

And it is catching, though probably not so much for Declan, who has stronger antibodies against this kind of contagion.

Noyers-sur-Serein turned out to be the charm of the day, partly because we strayed into lovely secret countryside which we wouldn't have seen if the competent voice of the sat nav had been guiding us.

Steve told Declan: "I bet you forgot that sat nav again. Really, when you go home you'll have to look into those memory lapses you're suffering from."

We walked around this quaint little village which was like a museum, a picture of a time gone by. Swallows swooped by the wooden alcoves underneath the chiselled stone of the timber buildings. They must have been building their nests inside these open stone arches since they were constructed in the fifteenth century. The curves and semicircles of the arches shielded a full view of what lay beyond them and that gave the village a teasing air of mystery. The cobbled streets were uneven beneath our feet which made us – Treasa and me anyway – grateful we weren't in high heels.

Though there was a good choice of restaurants, they were all busy and we had to wait until someone had vacated a table. That meant killing quite a lot of time because the French have a habit of lingering over Sunday lunch, a noon to evening affair, a day for the family, Uncle Tom Cobley and all, and dog, the essential French accessory. I never know how the French manage to get past the hygiene laws laid down by Brussels but I would say if you were to refuse a dog his place underneath a table in a French restaurant, you could forget his owner's custom for evermore. And they don't suffer any adverse affects. They live longer than most – the people I mean. Maybe the dogs do too, for all I know. There are no statistics that I'm aware of for that. But really, French longevity has probably more to do with the special way they relax over a meal or with their first-class health system rather than having dogs underneath the table.

In restaurants well-behaved French children are noticeable, so much so that it became the subject of a book: *French Children Don't Throw Food*. The author, Pamela Druckerman, concludes that one of the reasons for this is that French parents don't tiptoe around their children as much as in the Anglo Saxon world. They eat what adults eat, without a murmur or without running around and annoying every other client in the restaurant. A book could also be written on how well French dogs behave themselves in restaurants. There's not a bark out of them, not a whine; they hardly stir from underneath the table. I do wonder at times where I went wrong but if I were to bring my little mutt to a restaurant, there's no way she would lie beneath the table and be satisfied with just a bowl of water while the rest of us ate and drank merrily.

It was getting late by the time we finished lunch, so our look around Avallon on the way back to the hotel was hasty. I liked the steepness of this town, the way the long terraced gardens, lush with several shades of vegetables, swept down to the road's edge. Their owners lived higher up the hill, and you caught a fleeting glimpse of the backs of the houses, which looked a lot more homely than the view you get from the front. People were doing the things they do in the back: hoeing the weeds, hanging out the washing, playing with the dog. It was all very lovely, the half-seen view, unspoiled by full knowledge as we sped past. It fuels the imagination, recalls the lulling childhood joy of the half-known, the half-heard murmur of adult conversation, the half-deciphered words that go on and on and on. How was there always something more to say, no matter how much adults had already said?

Avallon is an old place. The principal north-south Roman road that linked Lyon to Boulogne once passed by here. Being on the main thoroughfare brought its own woes and this town endured much in the layers of wars of Saracens, Normans, English, French. For the same reason, it seems, with all the passers by, Avallon was badly hit by the Bubonic plague of the mid fourteenth century. Another variant of a Roman road cut through Quarré-les-Tombes across Morvan and this was the road we took next morning.

In the early hours, before the dew of dawn had a chance to rise and wipe the fields dry, we set off by narrow, winding roads, past the low-lying villages and the midsummer scents of Morvan. The French word for dew – *la rosée* – was just right for the scene. It's a word that rolls and floats. That morning it whispered and glistened and painted a picture obscure and laden.

It was hard to separate past from present at this dim witching hour. The damp morning fields looked as if they were drenched in the wine the Romans brought to these parts, or obscured in the fog of their steam rooms, thermal spas and gyms. All that was missing were the statues of Bacchus they built here in honour of their god of wine.

Morvan is a territory within a territory, of woodland and granite, a wild outcrop in the middle of the rich limestone land of Burgundy. It was a main stronghold of the Resistance movement during World War II, and you could well see why, because the place is dense with heaths, bracken and forests. It would be hard to find a better place to hide and fight the enemy.

Layers of settlers put down roots here, from hunter to Celt, to Roman, to Christian, Saracen and Viking. The Celts made their journey here from Central Europe, between the eighth and seventh centuries BC, and Celtic traces stayed in the myths and legends. The name Morvan itself is Celtic for black mountain. But they left no written account of themselves. The knowledge of the passing bards remained jealously guarded in oral form, in poems accompanied by music. Maybe this very secrecy makes it feel like their wisdom still rises from the depths of the soil around here. Then the Romans came, bringing statues of their gods and emperors. Next Christians arrived and imposed their own ways. They gathered the remains of the saints, their bones, their hair, drops of their blood. These relics carried such wondrous powers that no monastery was without a good supply. Their most magical power of all was their great pull for pilgrims. Where there were pilgrims there was money.

Martin was the saint most linked to the conversion of the country folk and he was said to have been in Avallon in 376. It seems he did his share of breaking up of statues of false Roman gods but he is better remembered for splitting his cloak in two to share with a beggar. It's a tale full of warmth. That may be why so many churches in France are dedicated to him. It probably appeals to the principle of equality that coils its way through French tradition.

We drove on by this looping land of creeks and streams, the nearest mountainous region to Paris. Three rivers – the Yonne, the Cousin and the Cure – thread through Morvan, winding, conducting from the mountaintop the otherworldly energy with which this place is so charged, draining it down to the valleys beneath. The job of watercourses must surely have been to pull the ambience of heaven from its height so that we could all have a share in it.

These rivers served a practical use too. In the nineteenth century landlords profited from floating firewood to Parisians on the many networks of rivers and lakes. But for the majority life was tough. With two sources of natural wealth – water and forest, neither great job providers – this wild land drove the locals out, just as it draws tourists in today. Women found work supplying their milk to the babies of the rich families in Paris and other big cities. Companies like Cherut-Lemonnier in Paris did a lively business recruiting wet-nurses for the rich. They went to live with their employers, leaving their own children in the care of grandmothers. Other Morvan women nursed the children from government orphanages in their homes.

Now Morvan's income comes from tourism. It's a nature park criss-crossed with walking and hiking trails, It was turned into a national heritage site when François Mitterand was president of the Nièvre department. Nièvre was part of the area he represented in parliament – one of the four departments out of which Morvan cuts a slice. This was his favour to the region he represented for over two decades.

We planned to be in Vendée by evening and when Steve said he wanted to stop at just one last place, Vézelay, before we left Morvan, our first reaction was, *do we have to?* In the end we were grateful to him because Vézelay became the highlight. Treasa was really taken by the visit. She said when we were leaving, there's truth in the quote "Chance is God; choice is man."

But Steve reminded her that it didn't apply here. "It might have been chance for you but it was choice for me. I did a lot of reading on Vézelay before I left."

"Then it was chance that made you read about it, can't you see?" said the wry Declan.

In any case, the place where chance or choice or whichever had brought us to, appeared suddenly against the horizon as the road swept uphill and around to the right. That was our first sighting of Vézelay – a row of houses sitting on a hilltop, rising upwards towards the summit of a far-distant mount, glistening as the rooftops caught the early sun's rays. Few moments could compare with that one. Hauntingly beautiful it was, an instant that sent a rush of childhood sensations fountaining through you. As the road snaked uphill through countryside that soared and tumbled, Vézelay disappeared and reappeared in the gaps of hedgerows, limiting us to short glimpses at a time.

The day was heating up by the time we got there. We parked the car at the foot of the hill and walked the journey upwards on sloping cobbles, passing by terraced houses with deep basements cut into the hill. Some were built in the twelfth century, after a fire ravaged the village. As you climb, you feel the rising rhythm of the place, a kind of rhapsody of solidarity connecting you with the succession of people who have climbed this hill to their temple, to do the things they did to satisfy their need for ritual – light a fire, sacrifice a body, build a monastery, walk in procession after a holy relic, or whatever.

The monastery in Vézelay had one of the most prized relics, the body of Mary Magdalene, although the best part of this story is that when another claim to her body was made by a church in Saint Baume in Provence, Vézelay responded by saying, "Ah yes, you might have had it, but years ago our monks stole it and now it's ours."

Mary Magdalene was in great demand. Her special appeal was that she was a sinner like the rest of us. If ever anyone would, she should have had an insight into human frailty. And her waywardness didn't earn her punishment. Far from it. She became the chosen one, the special friend of Jesus, the one to whom he appeared first after his resurrection. So a lot of people wanted her attention so that they too might learn the knack of jumping the queue on the ones who were good all along. Heaven, if you notice, gives no reward for consistency. Take for example the labourers who came late to the vineyard and were paid the same as the ones who had toiled all day.

We're not into that kind of stuff nowadays, of the last being first and the first being last. Trade unions wouldn't stand for it. We have names for people who jump the queue, get what they haven't earned, words that never appeared in the gospels – freeloaders, spongers, wasters.

In any case, devotion to Mary Magdalene was already widespread in France from the early decades of the eleventh century. Several churches were built in her honour. The many mentions of Mary in the gospel were conveniently lumped together under the identity of Mary Magdalene: Mary the sinner who washed the feet of Jesus with her tears, Mary the sister of Lazarus, Mary at the foot of the cross. And the crowds came to visit her relic in their droves, swelling to bursting point on 22 July, her feast day.

The sweet magic of Vézelay was at its purest at the top of the hill. It was where the air breathed light and fragrant, and the spirit of the place was at its most potent. The view was rounded and steep, cascading, dipping and then levelling off. The basilica on top is a gem of a building, ornate but not showy. It faces east and catches the summer solstice with such precision that the sun's midday rays lance the centre of the nave. Churches faced east because that was where paradise was thought to be, towards the rising sun.

This place has received some special guests in its time and it feels so much like the keeper of tradition and history that it wouldn't be surprising if you heard that their ghosts still roam the place. On Easter Day 1146 the brilliant cavalcade of Louis VII, the King of France and his Queen, Aliénor, made their way up the hill. It was the eve of the Second Crusade. Bernard of Clairvaux, considered a saint even in his lifetime, stirred up the zeal of the vast throngs from the side of the hill, to take up arms against the cheeky Turks who had invaded Palestine and the holy city of Jerusalem. You couldn't imagine a better place to make a plea to a crowd, because the terrain slopes into a natural amphitheatre.

The event was timely in its boost, not just for Vézelay, but for Mary Magdalene, because by the mid twelfth century she was suffering a certain amount of elbowing out by her rival, Saint

Jacques-de-Compostela. Vézelay was a special assembly point on the journey to Compostela. It was on the main pilgrim route from Notre Dame in Paris and a meeting point for pilgrims from Poland, Hungary and Germany.

Even the twenty-one-year-old Queen Aliénor, though not normally a fan of Bernard's, was taken with his words and went on the crusade with the King. It was not unusual for women to take the cross with their husbands, and in any case she had a crusading tradition in the family. Her grandfather Guillaume IX of Aquitaine, the Duke Troubadour, was a famous crusader and her father's youngest brother, Raymond of Poitiers, was installed as Prince of Antioch.

Louis came back from the Crusade with more problems on his plate than before he left. Not only was the whole thing a shambles, an outing of bloodshed and military failure, but he and the Queen rowed strenuously. Rumour had it that she cheated on him with her handsome uncle, Raymond.

About forty years later the Kings of France and England led off the Third Crusade from Vézelay and in 1988, to keep up a long tradition, François Mitterand and Helmet Kohl climbed the hill as a gesture of reconciliation between their countries.

It would have been nice to be there to see the church steeping itself in midday light but we couldn't delay that long. We just stayed for one of the chanting sessions by the blue and white nuns from the order of the Fraternity of Jerusalem, nuns and monks who chant the praises of God three times a day. Their singing filled the church, and you fancied that there was an unbroken thread linking their song and the poems of the Celtic bards.

Before we left we visited the shrine of Mary Magdalene, braving the damp smell of the church crypt. On our way back Treasa bought a book on Vézelay, in French.

The saleswoman wondered if she had heard her right.

"In French?" she checked.

"Yes," Treasa confirmed.

"Are you able to read in French?" she asked again.

The question could have been taken as, *Fancy that, you can read in French though you speak it so badly.* I think that was the way Treasa took it up, because she answered the woman curtly.

As we got into the car once again, I felt a strange reluctance to go, like leaving home and facing the big world. Treasa said she had the same feeling.

It was a place where the reach of eroding time had touched lightly and where the past had yielded its own harvest. The joy of finding it when we didn't expect to made it all the sweeter and we thanked Steve for letting us freeload on his work. Of course it wasn't fair that we came at the last hour and got the same enjoyment out of his diligent research but it must have been OK because we had the evidence of the good book to prove it.

# CHAPTER 8

As we drove away from Vézelay the road twisted and meandered as if it was conspiring not to let us go. The day was expansive; it soared over the passing hills and uplands, past brown and green grasses and mosses. We all agreed that it was nice not to have to go straight on to the highway until the strange spirit of Morvan had washed off. We drove along at a leisurely pace, by open country and small villages.

Then, all of a sudden, the driver announced that we were low on petrol. He said it so casually that none of us thought much about it. He has that habit, Declan, of saying a serious and a trivial thing in much the same tone. So we thought it was a simple matter of buying some along the way. But as we passed by farmland, hills, more farmland, more hills, a village and yet another village with not a sign of a shop, not to mention a petrol station, the mood shifted and the beauty of the landscape began to take on a look of non-beauty.

Blaming the driver isn't fair at all, but fairness isn't what comes to mind when you're about to be stranded in the middle of nowhere. Some of the criticism was justified. Good and all as Declan is at reading maps, he has a habit of leaving it till the very last minute to refill the tank. He knows exactly how far he can get after the yellow light first flashes to warn that fuel is low. I think it's a game for him. But it was a game we didn't fancy playing that day. What if we were caught, on roads so narrow that it would be impossible, not to mention unsafe, to walk?

Treasa, normally in top form when she's being driven along a country road, was leaning forward looking straight ahead, her worried face in her hands. All Steve's light-heartedness had dried up. Declan was saying nothing, which made him look twice as guilty. All our heads were tilted towards the petrol gauge, trying to get a side view of it, as if looking at it would help to squeeze more mileage out of it. I suggested slowing down might save fuel but that was overruled by the driver, who said that, on the contrary, it used more. From then on, we all looked nervously at every corner which had to be taken at a slower pace. We listened to the changing hum of the engine and imagined each drop of fuel turning to vapour. A kind of compound worry was building up – a group worry – worry multiplied by four, because if enjoyment is transferable, so is its opposite.

As the tetchiness intensified, Declan said, "Well you know buying petrol is a simple job. It can be done by anyone. And the petrol gauge isn't a secret. It's there for anyone to read."

"True. But we did say that whoever was driving should look after the petrol," said Treasa. "That was one of our first agreements, that whoever was driving could choose the music but also had to watch the petrol."

"That means you never have to look after the petrol at all because you never drive," said Declan.

"Then you should have brought that up when we were making the rule in the first place and you do choose the music. You stick to that side of the deal all right," she argued.

"What are we doing arguing about music for goodness sake," snapped Steve.

Another garageless village passed by, another, yet another. It was endless.

Then, out of nowhere, what was that we saw before us? A sign – SUPER U… MINUTES AHEAD. None of us caught the number of minutes. The Super U chain of supermarkets has a habit of putting signs up a long distance ahead of their location, but the estimated number of minutes to get there is often more appropriate for those travelling by jet.

Please, please let it be soon, we prayed. Most Super U supermarkets sell petrol, but not all. None of us really believed that prayer could move a petrol station, especially when the problem was caused by human failing, but it was worth a try.

Then another sign appeared: SUPER U, TWO MINUTES. You could hear the united exhalation of sighs.

Treasa slumped back into her seat with a thud of relief. "Two minutes, even if it's exaggerated, could be walked," she said.

But our troubles were not over. Would this Super U sell petrol? And if it did, would it be open? It was now five minutes past one o'clock. We all knew how lunchtime in France could go on until three in the afternoon. French supermarkets have been taking the lead in changing the tradition of the midday shutdown. It's a shame really. It spoils the leisurely pace, but please, please let just this Super U operate according to the rules of raw capitalism, just this once. They can sit down for lunch for as long as they like everywhere else. They can denounce capitalism, as only the French can, some other time.

Joy oh joy, it was open, gloriously open. And they sold petrol. The sheer delight of it, relief multiplied by four. It was better than the loveliest scene. We filled our tank abundantly. And when it was full we felt like filling it even more. Never again would we run out of petrol. It was going to be the responsibility of all four of us from now on. Treasa was clearly embarrassed at how willing she had been to pass on the blame when things went wrong. And really Declan didn't deserve it, because he is fairness itself. He might be none too quick to apportion praise but neither does he indulge in dishing out blame.

"You're right," Treasa said guiltily. "I should take my turn in checking the petrol."

He just smiled and said dryly: "As long as you don't offer to take your turn driving, that's OK."

She doesn't always like to be reminded that her driving can threaten her own and everyone else's existence, but this time she took it well. I expect she knew she had earned it.

"I didn't hear much about this theory of yours about chance being God and choice being man when we were nearly stranded in the middle of green fields a few minutes ago," quipped Steve.

"Oh what a great comedian you are. In fact we passed by lovely countryside. It would have been nice to see where we crossed the Yonne River," she said, taking a look at the map.

"Would you like me to go back and let you enjoy it, then?" asked Declan, in a strong air of sarcasm.

Problems can only be laughed at when seen from afar and though our bad form hadn't yet receded too far into the distance, we had a laugh at how easily a good drive can be spoiled. By negligence, was it, on someone's part, not mentioning names or looking at anyone in particular? Let's just put it down to group culpability this time.

We were soon on the main road towards Orleans – highway country – driving by the elbow of the Loire. There was no shortage of places where you could buy petrol now. We had left behind the deep and leafy world of strange powers and magic virtues – and garageless villages – and we were passing by huge unfenced cornfields, great commercial enterprises of farms.

Mainland France was divided into ninety-six departments (with a further four overseas) following the Revolution, in an effort to get away from the kind of centralized control that royal power was associated with. Each department has its own local elected government, in contrast to the old royal appointments and bought offices. The shape of the departments, like the ancient provinces they replaced, was guided by nature: mountains, rivers and other natural boundaries. All of them were arranged so that they would be roughly the same size, small enough for someone to reach the department's capital town in a day's journey. This evokes such a pastoral image, reaching the capital town at your ease, a slow-hoofed journey or stepping it out on your own two feet.

We drove across the countryside, from Orleans, Tours, Angers. At Angers we turned south towards Cholet, driving by the *bocage* of Vendée, which consists of small holdings. *Bocage* is a feature of where

Celtic influence was deepest and most enduring. Big industrial farming, like we had passed earlier, never located itself here, because the land wasn't rich enough. Most fields were probably smaller than five acres. Where the ground rose you could see a patchwork of enclosures rambling into the distance, hedged into rectangles, streaked and furrowed. It's a landscape that recalls tightly meshed memories of modest farming, a simple life, a place where customs were observed, where fields had names, where the earth has felt the tread of the feet of generations of the same families, not like in the big collectivised fields further north, where only the roll of machine wheels has been felt for decades.

This terrain holds memories of war too. The dense foliage of the *bocage* shielded the Vendéen rebels while they launched guerrilla assaults and hit-and-run attacks against the Republican government in 1793. Vendéen farmers had sided with the King and paid the price for their sedition. The French revolutionaries had rebelled against authority, and this defiance struck a romantic chord. But when the Vendéen rebels thought they would do the same – strike out at the new power – it had not quite the same romantic resonance. They were put down in a violent massacre. The rebels were no match for the armies of the Republic. As they advanced northwards, they lost their best assets – the coverage of the undergrowth and the support of the locals. In the early months of 1794 Republican armies followed a "pacification" policy, a nice name for crushing the insurgents. Twice as many peasants and workers went to the scaffold as members of the nobility and the middle classes.

Though peasants didn't support the Republicans, they gained from the Revolution. Feudalism was abolished. Tithes and hunting rights were made more favourable and the landlords' claim on the peasants' production was weakened.

Passing through Vendée you can still see it is a region that has held on to the old ways rather like the marshes and sodden moorlands of the region hold on to their moisture. The cross of Calvary stands guard over several T-junctions, lone country chapels are dotted here and there, statues of the Virgin Mary are recessed into the walls of some of the old farmhouses. Monuments commemorate war too. The Vendéen wars were, among other things, a Christian struggle against secular Republicanism and urban values.

The traditional Vendéen farmhouse is half single-storey, half two-storey. Holiday home developments have kept faithful to this design. But though it looks well in individual houses, when it's replicated a few hundred fold, it loses its charm.

Herds of lean cows, the colour of Vendée's beaches, grazed in the low-lying pastures. Gardeners, mostly older men, were bent over hoes, tending their vegetable plots. They were laid out neatly, ruler straight, with not a weed in sight. Further west, towards the coast, where grasslands got tougher and clover was scarce, cattle had to seek among the reeds and rushes to find some sweet blades of grass. Like the people, French cattle are foodies and they leave this marshy land to those who are not bothered by its rough growth – the bog lark, the snipe, the curlew and the bittern. Green Venice is the name Vendéen tourism gives to the rectangles of salinated water near the coast. It's a good name. It conjures visions of leisurely cruising on Venetian waters but the weather is a little cooler this distance north of Venice.

Declan began to read out a litany of Vendée's famous sons:

"François Rabelais, whose monastery was in Fontenay-le-Comte, set a lot of the adventures of his giant, Gargantua, around this region. Cardinal Richelieu was Bishop of Luçon. The physician Ferchault de Réaumur, inventor of the mercury thermometer, lived in Vendée and Richard the Lionheart spent some time in the Pays des Olonnes. The little coastal cottage where Clemenceau, "The Tiger", retired to is… "

"OK, OK, later we can see all the places where those famous men lived but what about now? I'm starving," Treasa cut in, evidently feeling our problems were more immediate than those men and in any case I think she was secretly irritated that no women of renown were listed.

We couldn't agree on where to eat. A recommended restaurant

in the seaside village of Brétignolles-sur-mer didn't work out. Declan was the only one among us who really cared for meat. The menu displayed on the window offered meat for starters, meat for main course, meat for... well, not quite meat for dessert. Considering the restaurant looked out to sea, there was surprisingly little fish on offer. We were tired and cranky.

"We're ready to eat one another so there's hardly any need to go to a restaurant at all," said Steve.

We took a walk by the sea, that great pacifier of the weary and the irascible. Brétignolles has no shortage of pathways for walkers and bikers, winding along by the sandy coastline.

The weather is usually good in Vendée but it takes the whims of the Atlantic in the face. The day's heat remained in the evening though the blazing sun was beaten back by gathering clouds. The sun wasn't going to do its showpiece that evening. Summer sunsets here bring walkers to a halt. They stand in groups to gaze as it slips spectacularly away for the night. That evening looked as if it was shaping up for a different kind of display. A stillness hung in the air, the kind that precedes a thunder storm. Each step felt as if you had weights in your shoes.

The sandy footpath was alive with a collection of species. Maybe it was the humidity that brought them out in such force. Ants were busily working in unison on the sandy path. A few lizards bolted in front of us. They were luminous green, as if they had stolen the colour out of the sunburnt grass. Every now and then a grey one darted forward but they were in the minority. Sand-flies with translucent wings hopped lightly around our feet. They were all combing the path for what, I couldn't make out, but they looked mighty busy. Large insects were buzzing around us, making a noise like a light engine. They looked as if they might tangle themselves in someone's hair. I reckoned they would find Treasa's more attractive to get lost in than mine because she has thick frizzy hair, so I felt safe enough.

Steve was looking nervous, no doubt concerned about his drawing power for insects. I asked a man who was walking his dog what they were called. He didn't know but he assured us they were harmless. I was tempted to say they might be harmless for some but he should meet our friend with his built-in magnet for flying creatures.

Brétignolles's coast from Marais-Girard to La Sauzaie is well stocked with rock. Having to fight their corner against the ravages of the ocean, they have braced themselves into appropriate shapes, jagged and gnarled, sharp as a monster's tooth. Sometimes this outcrop of stone is dotted with mussel-pickers, buckets in hand, balancing themselves as they search between the cracks in the stones for something for dinner. But there was no one out that evening.

The rocks on the seafront formed miniature bays at the water's edge. Some of the inlets were as straight as canals. Pools of water higher up in scooped-out hollows on the rocks stood as proof of the height the waves had reached earlier that day. And the water rested there, laid back and stagnant, relaxing in its containers, as it watched the hardworking breakers, spitting and foaming on the knife-edged stone, angry at having to do all the work.

The waves of time have eaten into the stone, making some dagger-like, while lapping and chiselling others smooth. Some are honed into curious shapes, like natural monuments. Persistent water and yielding stone together sure can make nifty artwork. If the leaning pyramid of Rock Sainte-Véronique had been shaped by the hand of man, it could not have bettered what the repeated assaults of the ocean have done. It must be one of the most photographed stones around here – Brétignolles's touristic ambassador. May the waves wash lightly on it and keep it in its present shape.

Giving rocks names, Creux du Renard, La Roche Trouée, Rock Sainte-Véronique, fits into Vendée's legendary tradition. Folktales around these parts have seafaring themes of sirens, mermaids and fishermen. Christian and pagan ideas are mixed with the real and the fanciful. But, above all, Vendée's legends are moralising tales. Some are warnings to people who go against nature, or those who defy the social code. Women who cheat on their husbands pay the price. They might be washed out to sea or changed into an animal. Nothing so terrible, that I know of, befalls a man who does the same.

"Fancy that," said Treasa in mock surprise. "The code was different for the two then?"

It certainly was, and not just in Vendéen legends. France was no trailblazer when it came to equality for women. A woman could never inherit the throne of France. And after monarchy was brought to an end, the new Republican regime took its time to equalise the genders. Some put the blame on Rousseau's influence. He saw women as delightful creatures, but none too gifted when it came to rational thought. A very popular book in its day (the late eighteenth century) was *Système Physique et Morale de la Femme* by Pierre Roussel, and he saw a woman's role as bearing and caring for children.

Republican France didn't economize on the statues of the *Marianne,* the feminine symbol of the Revolution, but when it came to doing something practical for the real woman, any ideas on equality were stopped in their tracks. When French suffragettes protested in the late nineteenth century, the newspaper *Le Figaro* asked whether after women, cattle were going to be given the vote. This great favour was not granted until April 1944 and French women participated for the first time in elections in 1945. A decade later an appeal court judge said that, in his opinion, women, without exception, would be unsuited to authority. And besides, female judges would damage the prestige of the judiciary. France still has a low proportion of women members of parliament.

With so many other things to do, there was no point in spending precious holiday time brooding over history. The following day we hired bikes to see some of Vendée's coastline. The man in Le Goeland Bleu in Brétignolles, a friendly family bike-hire business, adjusted the saddle so many times for Treasa that Steve asked her was she thinking of cycling the whole two hundred kilometres of Vendée's coastline. We cycled to Saint-Gilles-Croix-de-Vie, ten kilometres away, hardly marathon stuff but we were pleased with ourselves.

We waited for the heat of day to settle before setting off on our expedition. There was a stillness about the evening glow that made you feel flush with childhood feelings. The sun's low angle elongated our shadows and made cartoon-like shapes of our bike wheels. A fresh sea breeze kept us pleasantly cool as we clipped along. Drunk-looking trees shaded the cycle path along the way, their trunks bent and deformed by the constant Atlantic drafts whipping past their legs. Every now and then a burst of bird-song broke out of the thicket, but the singers kept well out of view. A flock of birds flew overhead, black against the sky, in a single current of air. They made a swooping change of route, in a unity that would have put Napoleon's armies to shame, and then they glowed against the sun rays, revealing that they were white, not black. How light brings things into existence. Scent does too. Aromas floated our way, though when you tried to get a second inhalation of the perfume, it stayed stubbornly aloof. It was playing the tantalising game of firsts: like the first cup of tea tastes better than the second, or the first blast of love. When you try to recapture it, it's somehow not so available.

The sound of woodpigeons filled the evening. They cut off teasingly in mid coo. Steve said, "Someone caught them trying to sing and they were so embarrassed by their poor voices that they cut off without warning."

There was a covering of netting over most of the coastline pathways, to protect them from eroding under the weight of feet and bike wheels. It's a popular place to walk dogs. And it's a popular practice not to clean up after them. It catches in the netting and then it gets tracked everywhere. I think no fine is too great for dog owners like that.

We reached the Vie River and accompanied it all the way to Saint-Gilles-Croix-de-Vie, and when we saw the high apartment blocks of this fishing harbour you would think we had seen the domes of Moscow. We're not what champions are made of.

We took a walk around the town. It was festooned with funnel-shaped flowers of pinks, reds and yellows – the kind you see on picture postcards, growing high and slender out of the tiniest crack between concrete footpaths and the walls of houses. I wondered what they were called so I asked a man on the street.

"*Rose trémière,*" he told me. The English translation is Althaea but they are more commonly known as Hollyhock. He said he had taken seeds and planted hundreds of them around the town. He could give us some, he offered. So we walked back with him to his house. It was a fairly long walk. After a while the men began to wonder why they were walking so far just for flower seeds that they weren't interested in, so they arranged to meet us up the town later and Treasa and I went with him to his neat terraced cottage, which stepped onto the footpath. As he opened the door he revealed a small hallway of glossy ceramic tiles. Treasa was so taken with the tiles that the seeds became secondary. She asked him where he had bought them and I was wondering for a minute if she was proposing to buy some and bring them home. She has a habit sometimes, when she spots something she fancies, of insisting on loading it into any free space that's left in the car, and you end up going home with several items under your feet, on your lap, or on your head if it could be done.

The man filled two plastic yogurt containers with seeds. We thanked him abundantly. And when we joined the men later Treasa talked of the fate of having asked that man about the flowers. "Of all the people in this town whom we could have asked, fancy that it was the very person who had such an interest in these flowers."

"That was a coincidence right enough," said Steve.

She corrected him: "No it was not a coincidence. There's no such thing."

"What was it then?" he asked

"Destiny" answered Declan, having a joke on her.

"Choice is God, chance is man," said Steve.

"Very funny," Treasa said. "And you don't even have it right. It's chance is God; choice is man."

But the best of it all was, when we planted the seeds they never grew. Maybe they were making a protest – keeping a French custom alive – at having been uprooted from their native home and planted in damp and colder Ireland.

# CHAPTER 9

I wouldn't consider a visit to Vendée complete without crossing to the island of Noirmoutier. To call it an island at all is a bit of a cheat because it has two links to the mainland: a bridge and the *gois*. Crossing by the bridge, elegant and all as it is, doesn't have the same allure as going by the *gois*, because you feel you're using a method of getting to this island that has been stepped out since the beginning of time. Even the word itself, *gois*, hums of survival because it was one of the few words from the local dialect that managed to live through the linguistic onslaught to make Parisian French the national standard, following the Revolution. And it is much more natty than its English counterpart, causeway. It comes from the local verb *goiser*, which means walking while getting your shoes wet.

Not so long ago France was a country of several dialects: Breton, Corsican, Catalan, Basque, Occitan and a host of others. In the 1850s only one in five people spoke French. In the south they spoke the *langue d'oc*, the dialect of Provence. Northerners spoke the *langue d'oïl*, the dialect of the Paris region, and it was this that was chosen to become the national language. It was forcibly spread by Abbot Grégoire during Robespierre's Reign of Terror. His aim was to wipe out local dialects, which in his view were not just treacherous but also coarse and superstitious.

Nowadays, the big drive is against English. There's no policy to spread English. It's worse in a way. It's a silent takeover by the language of capitalism, and the idea of naked profiteering is something the French dislike in any case. The Académie Française is the official guardian of the French language, a kind of linguistic police of forty members (mainly male). One of its roles is to keep the language pure from foreign tainting and it puts a lot of effort into keeping out Anglicisms. It has some battle on its hands. Many French multinationals now use English at board meetings, in official documents and Anglicisms in advertising.

We were going to drive across the *gois,* of course. However romantic the local dialect may sound, we were going to draw the line at getting our shoes wet. We took our place in the queue about an hour before the tide sucked the water out, where two currents of sea meet and divide at low tide. Warning signs about crossing this 4,200-metre-long passage were placed here and there: *Risque de noyade* (Risk of drowning), *Parc de stationnement submersible* (submersible car-park). I hadn't thought of it as such a dangerous venture until I read them. It reminded me of the safety instructions before you begin a boat or a plane journey – where the emergency exits are, how to get into your life jacket – a moment of minor panic. But really the message they want to get to you in Noirmoutier is that the tide is not something to be trifled with.

In record time the currents went their separate ways, like a minor Red Sea parting. A broad strand, ridged and streaked, appeared where the disappearing waters had vacated. Instantly it was covered with a crowd in colourful wellies and raincoats filling their buckets with whatever fish the parting waters had not taken with them. Shrieking seagulls tried to beat the humans in the race for seafood.

You have a limited amount of time in which to make the crossing.

"I wonder what they'd do with you if you got a breakdown half way across," said Steve. He answered his own question: "That, I presume, is your problem. Shrug, shrug. Or what if your friends in the car behind you stalled? That would really put your friendship to the test."

It's not so funny. Some have been taken in the rising tide. About forty people have lost their lives between 1900 and 1982. Not so many, as statistics go. And, the book I had on Noirmoutier said that these were people who had not taken the recommended care. It says that victims got on too late and "were taken by surprise at the speed of the oncoming tide." (That last piece of information must surely have been only assumed.) The funniest story of rescue was that of a small group of musicians who got caught in rising tides in 1822. They took refuge on one of the buoys along the *gois*. The best way to attract attention, they found, was to perform a quick concert on the buoy. It was a funny course of action. Maybe they decided they would go out singing, leave the world doing what they liked best. We followed the rules rigidly – an hour and a half before and after low tide – our musical abilities wouldn't be up to taking any chances.

Paving work was done on the *gois* in the 1930s during two daily two-hourly sessions – day and night – the limited working shift that the tide allowed. But this passageway was used long before it was paved. Locals had been bringing animals across to the mainland at low tide for centuries. The first mention of the *gois* appeared during the time of Louis XIV. Vauban, the King's chief military architect, took a keen interest in Noirmoutier. He wasn't the first to spot the strategic value of this island with its northern tip facing the mouth of the Loire. Vikings, Saracens, Spaniards, English and Dutch had eyed up the place before him.

The *gois* was important to the Vendéens who revolted against the Republic. Their leader, François de Charette, used it to lead two thousand men through on the night of 29 September 1793. But his enemies took his example four months later, retook Noirmoutier and forced the Vendéen insurgents to lay down their arms. Republicans didn't spare the rebels. Nearly two thousand of them were executed, even though their own commander-in-chief called for clemency.

A cross called La Croix du Magnificat was erected in memory of the last of the rebel victims, on the spot where twenty-two people, mostly women, were executed on 16 Thermidor (the second month of the summer quarter of the new Republican calendar) of 1793. But it was no longer 1793. It was Year II of the Republic. (When it came to change Republicans meant business; it was to be of the root and branch sort. The calendar would no longer be related to the birth of Christ but to the birth of the Republic.) The condemned, chained in twos, made their way from the château where they had been held prisoner, to their place of execution, singing the Magnificat. I think this story binds together beautifully Vendéen piety and the French spirit of defiance. The Magnificat spoke the language of sedition – how the Lord had put down the mighty from their seat and exalted the humble. The Republicans had a problem with that. They had already put down the mighty from their seat. Once was enough to turn the world on its head. And so the rebels were put to death. They were the last victims of the revolutionary tribunal, which came to an end after the fall of Robespierre in 1794. Charette himself was executed with great pomp on 26 March 1796, in the town square in Nantes.

Today Noirmoutier is a place without airs or pretensions. It bears the look of a working island, laid-back, at ease with itself. It doesn't over push its tourist credentials. Winding around the island on the little tourist train we viewed the great expanse of landscape with nothing to hinder the view because about a quarter of the island's surface is *marais* – swampy marshland from which salt is extracted. Where there is *marais*, the landscape is an expanse of flatness – no houses, no roads, no trees, no fences to obstruct the view, just a great breadth of salt-works constructed in orderly rectangles of brine.

Some of the vegetation makes it look as though a patch of southern France was transplanted to here. Plants like *arbousiers*, native to the Mediterranean, thrive happily because of the mildness of the weather on the island. Mimosa flowers flourish too at the end of January, as they do on the Mediterranean coast, which is why some call it the island of mimosa. Long gone are the days when salt was Noirmoutier's main product. Today potatoes get the prize. They are smooth and fine tasting and are in much demand in Parisian restaurants. The mild weather – frost and snow are very rare – means they can produce three crops a year.

*Bois de la Chaise* disrupts Noirmoutier's flatness with one hundred hectares of protected green oaks. Legend has it that a fairy changed the island's snakes into green oaks. When Republicans came to round up the Vendéen rebels they weren't worried about the fairy's curse, being enlightened men of reason. They nearly destroyed the green oaks, using them for firewood during the awful winters of 1792, 1793 and 1794 (or, sorry, years I, II and III of the Republic). Natural disaster caused even greater ruin. A cyclone hit on 13 February 1972 that knocked down four thousand trees in just half an hour. Probably it was the fairy coming back for vengeance.

We had lunch in Le Rafio. They do delicious salads, and when I asked the waitress how to marinade the peppers like they did, she gave me the recipe without the slightest hesitation. There was no jealous guarding of the secret of their skill, though I must admit when I tried it, mine were not nearly as good. Transplanting recipes works no better than transplanting *rose trémière*.

Alas, we found the tearoom behind the pâtisserie of Brigitte and Patrick Giraudet shut. We were all set, with dinner booked later than usual to allow for the planned tea and pâtisserie. How disappointing. I just had to describe their high-quality coffee, the wonderful assortment of teas, the old cast-iron oven, the family photographs of a long line of bakers and confectioners, the teasing half-glimpse of a flowery patio. The change of plan left us lingering on the pavement, wondering what to do with ourselves.

With our spare time we went to see the castle and the church. The castle, an old fortress, looks well for its age. It is one of France's oldest feudal citadels and is in an impressive state of repair, in spite of its share of assaults over the years. During the Revolution it served as a prison for rebellious Vendéens. During World War I it held interned foreigners. It now has a quieter role to play, as a museum.

The Church is dedicated to Saint Philbert. The monastery he founded in 674 lay on this spot, though only a part of the crypt remains. His body is here. As well as spreading the Christian Word, the monks exploited the land and harvested salt. Noirmoutier, which means black habit, got its name from the black clothes the monks wore.

The heart of Francis III de Trémoille, Lord of Noirmoutier, who died about four hundred years ago, is here too. Lords were very fond of leaving their hearts in local churches. There's hardly a church that doesn't hold the heart of some local noble or other. Back then they seemed equally fond of extracting the hearts of the dead as pulling out the hearts of fearful animals.

We couldn't reach agreement on whether to go to see where the old fishing village of Eloux once was. It vanished in the early nineteenth century when the dunes were mobile and before the pines were planted to stabilise the ground. Declan thought there was not much point in going to see a place that wasn't even there and it was hard to argue with that. Steve too thought we should take their word for the existence of this non-place. Its disappearance is explained by a legend, which shows the consequences for those who break the rules. This time the culprit was a man: Jean-Nez-au-vent, a local fisherman. He became enchanted by the sirens who used to hide behind the rocks near Eloux. Half fish, half woman, they were remarkably beautiful, with eyes the blue-green of the sea and long hair like seaweed (normally hair like seaweed wouldn't be desirable but it seems in this case it was). He stayed watching them later and later each evening. His wife, wild with jealousy, urged him to take one home. And he did, not realising what the plan for dinner was that evening. She popped the lovely siren into a pot of boiling water and cooked her. That night a terrible storm blew up and destroyed the village of Eloux to make sure everyone knew that you try this experimental cuisine at your peril. A tidal wave drowned all its inhabitants leaving nothing but a sand dune. And the sirens there still lament their beautiful companion.

That evening we dined in Château de la Vérie, near Challans, an old-world, daunting looking hotel, noted for its cuisine. Cooked siren was definitely not on the menu.

The day was fading as we made our way back to Brétignolles. It was that pleasing time of eventide that settles in the fading light when day and night start to merge. Spires of the approaching village churches rose over the fields and hillocks. Willowy trees along the roadside swayed and turned up their leaves, showing a silvery grey underside, like the petticoats of dancers catching the breeze of their dance. Where fields rose high, bales of hay climbed in black-plastic-covered rounds, as if they had taken on the shape of the wheels of the machinery that had harvested them. Cattle lumbered across the fields; others were lying, ruminating and lazing before nightfall. Further on, untilled and ungrazed, lay the prairie of *marais* for which Vendée is known.

We had planned to spend the next day in Poitiers but it turned out so hot that we went to the beach instead. Seas are wild around Brétignolles. There's a great choice of beaches but one is as angry as the other. As the waves come charging in, they spit and rant like a raging bull. But when they're challenged by the shore's edge their self-assured air deserts them and they swirl into a meek foam around your feet. They're like a symbol of the journey from young to old – the self-assured display life puts on in the full flush of youth comes off its virile pedestal as it crashes onto the shore of old age.

A sea of high waves is a whole lot more fun than calm waters. Everyone was jumping at the approaching breakers. The portion of sea marked off for lifeguard surveillance was packed. It would have been hard to swim among all those people even if the waves had allowed you to. Declan swam in past the crowds, beyond the breakers. The lifeguard did not let him out of the range of his watchful eye. Afterwards the four of us had a game of beach ball but it got too hot and so we decided to pursue a different pleasure. We went to the supermarket to choose some Vendéen wine.

You have to grab your chance to buy the local wine while you're in an area, because each locality promotes its own and once you move on, the wine of the previous region is hard to find. Vendée's wine has a good reputation. It even got the approval of France's popular King, Henry IV. The story goes that when he spent a few nights as a guest of the local noble in Château de Beaumarchais (which is two miles from Brétignolles, these days offering guest accommodation) he complained of the heat. His host offered him a *pichet* of the local wine to cool him down. The King drank it and reckoned it was an *excellent breuvage* (drink) that deserved recognition. That praise was much valued and the wines from these parts still do justice to the tribute of this sixteenth century monarch, though I doubt if his recommendation still influences sales.

Next day our trip to Poitiers was foiled when we ran into closed roads. What was going on, we asked a man who looked like as if he knew.

"The Tour de France," he said. Didn't we know?

There was no chance of getting through until two in the afternoon, at the earliest, he said. It was not yet ten. He showed us a map. We were enclosed in a circuit, inside which we could drive all we liked but we couldn't get beyond the boundaries. Cars were parked on both sides of the narrow road. It took about a twenty-five-point turn, with mirrors folded tightly on both sides, to get ourselves out of the spot.

And so we spent the morning driving by one small village after another, on roads lined by trees, passing by farmland, low-lying and luscious. Every now and again dappling sunbeams broke through the branches and lay on the road. Signs beckoned from farm gates, offering goat's cheese, fresh fruit, vegetables straight off the ridges, the freshest of eggs. Some of the charming places within the area in which we were caged were La Chapelle Hermier (which looks very medieval), Martinet, Beaulieu-sous-la-Roche. In Beaulieu there was a little pottery shop, with door wide open. When we went in no one was there. It was like someone had gone to lunch and left the door open. It was all very rustic, like a world abandoned, an Alice in Wonderland moment. We could have helped ourselves to the pottery, as far as you could see. There were no visible signs that they worried about theft, nothing so crude as CCTV. This kind of faith in humanity is quite common in rural France and is a sweet contrast to the padlocked world of urban life. We looked around at the bowls, candlesticks and other pottery wares, but even if we had wanted to buy some there was no way of paying.

On the village square we met a few people who had their journeys equally disrupted by the Tour de France, and a kind of solidarity built up between us fellow captives. One woman was holding a printout of the tour route. Her house was just a few yards on the far side of the boundary and that near-but-far feeling made it seem more of an inconvenience for her than for us. She tried to talk to Declan in English, with a woefully limited vocabulary. "How do you say *ville* in English?" she asked Treasa.

"Town."

That got her as far as the second next word when she had to ask again.

"How do you say *voiture?* How do you say *rouler*?"

Good on her for persevering. Treasa was helpful. I'm sure she was thinking of the many times she was in that kind of linguistic trouble herself.

Together we examined the map and after having looked at it this way and that, we concluded there was nothing for it but to relax and enjoy our few hours of captivity.

The woman with the limited English recommended a restaurant across the road. The place looked popular. I don't know if all the clients were locked up within the Tour de France enclosure but there were rather a lot of people having lunch in such a small village. Most of them looked like locals – a sign of a good restaurant. The *plat du jour* looked like a meat dish from the sparse residue on the plates.

"What are our chances of getting a fish dish?" Treasa wondered.

Not good, we agreed. Not much chance of getting a table either, and so we left and headed for Aizenay, where we ended up having a take-away meal bought in the Super U's hypermarché. By the time we had eaten, and had a look around the town, and bought some presents in the gift shop beside the church, our sentence was up and we were free once again to drive where we liked. We went back to Brétignolles and decided that the next day would, we hoped, be the day to visit Poitiers.

When I said that, in a strange way, I had enjoyed the day, the two men said mockingly, "Chance is God; choice is man"

"Indeed," agreed Treasa. "There's no joke about it. We'd never have seen all these little villages if we hadn't been hemmed in for half the day and I really found it all so pleasant." Then she added, in a bossy tone: "And I'm glad at least that you both got the quote right this time."

"Who was responsible for that little gem anyway?" asked Steve.

"It came from an Iris Murdoch novel," said Treasa.

"She has a lot to answer for," said Declan.

The quote was tailor-made for that day, for the thrill of the upset plan and being left at the mercy of chance. The shift from the carefully organised itinerary made Steve agree too, that the most enjoyable things in life are involuntary.

"OK, OK. If you all had such a wonderful day, why don't we just do it more often?" said Declan in mock tetchiness.

# CHAPTER 10

For a while we thought that destiny was scheming to keep us from Poitiers and we didn't believe it until this city's famous ramparts came within view. We drove up by the narrow streets and parked in the town centre. The driver in front of us had a camper van and he banged loudly into a beam at the entrance to the car park. He should have read the notice warning of the height limit. Width was no more generous. Cars were packed so tightly that mirrors had to be snapped into their narrowest position to fit between the tightly-drawn lines. Our mirrors were well flexed from the Tour de France crush the day before.

Everyone managed to squeeze out of the car though our clothes took the dust of the vehicles on either side. When Treasa complained, Steve asked her why she dresses in such fine clothes anyway, why does she not follow his example and rough it a bit. She gave him a look that suggested that definitely was not the solution to her problem.

In the tourist office tour guides were advertising their services. They were showing one site per morning. The Palais de Justice was the monument on view that day and that was going to take three hours. Treasa would have been happy to give it that amount of time because few places thrill her so much, but the rest of us weren't so committed even though this was once the seat of power of the Dukes of Aquitaine.

It was the great cultural hub of the south, where poets found patrons and where the first echoes of Europe's lyric poetry in the vernacular were heard. One of the things that made this court such a literary powerhouse was its position, on a trade route from the Mediterranean. Even at the height of Christian-Muslim warfare, commerce continued, and it is easy to see in the imagination the parading caravans of old transporting their wares from far-off markets, stopping in Poitiers before going further north. Exchange of goods led to exchange of ideas and stirring insights came to these parts from distant lands: architecture from Byzantium, philosophy from Greece, Arabic applied mathematics, enamelling, music, lyric poetry. Together they hummed here under the auspices of the local dukes.

We agreed to do a quick guideless tour of the Palais de Justice, much too hasty to give this ancient place its due. It's now used as a law court, and lawyers floated around in stiff collars and full length black attire, though no one wore a wig. But otherwise they looked as formal as the medieval Dukes of Aquitaine. The official hall of the palace was once the grand meeting place for the chief lords of the South and West of France. Treasa couldn't contain her delight at seeing the very castle where they lived, still in a usable state after all those centuries.

"When you think of how different life was then," she said. "Not a computer, nor a mobile phone in sight. I think it's all just mesmerising."

"Computer, did you say?" asked Declan. "Don't we well remember a world without computers ourselves?"

And so we do. Indeed we remember a whole lot of things, stretching back way beyond our liking.

Outside the palais there was a plaque to the most famous duke, Guillaume IX, the Troubadour. In his time – in the eleventh and twelfth centuries – musicians, singers and story tellers went from castle to castle, and the Duke was an enthusiastic host. He became their great patron and his court was the most refined in the West. We're told he spent time reading and writing when he wasn't busy at warfare (Aquitaine was notorious for its feuds). A crusader and man of letters himself, he wrote poems spoken to musical accompaniment on subjects like courtly love, sexual prowess, the joys of life, the passing of time, those sort of things. Eleven of these song-poems have survived.

The Duke's writings became an important model for the troubadour poets. Troubadour poetry flowered between the eleventh and thirteenth centuries. It was written in the *langue d'oc,* the Provençal dialect, but it mixed in other influences, like Arabic and Celtic oral traditions.

The troubadours celebrated the love of someone remote – the poet's adoration of a woman who was interested but tantalizingly beyond reach.

"The thing is," said Treasa, "unavailable love has a potency that fulfilled love never can have."

"Oh really?" Declan raised his eyebrows. And well he might look puzzled. They have been married for years.

But she stood firm. "Of course it is. How could you expect love spoiled by the humdrum toils of everyday life to hold its romance?"

He just shrugged, as if this alteration had happened without his notice.

The Duke Troubadour would have agreed. Perhaps the excitement of a crusade made it harder to stick to the humdrum life and after his return from the Holy Land he left his wife, Philippie, for the wife of one of his vassals, the Vicomte de Châtellerault. His writings became more gallant too, following the crusade. The thing was troubadour poetry often broke its own rules when the out-of-reach woman came within reach and it led to adultery. It was hardly the most surprising thing in the world. The Duke was excommunicated for his waywardness. The dispensation from sin so eagerly offered to crusaders willing to head off to the Holy Land didn't cover sins committed afterwards.

There were umpteen Guillaumes of Aquitaine: Guillaume the Pious, Guillaume the Young, Guillaume of the Iron Arm, Guillaume the Great, Guillaume the Troubadour. Guillaume X, the Toulousain (from Toulouse), was the last of the Guillaumes. He died during a pilgrimage to the tomb of Saint Jacques de Compostela, just a few kilometres from his destination. On his deathbed he named his eldest daughter, Aliénor, as his heir (the young Queen we had "met" in Vézelay). There is no one in the Middle Ages with whom so much legend has been associated (with the exception maybe of her son, Richard the Lionheart). Her father had left instructions that she marry the King of France. This would merge the family's extensive possessions around Poitiers with those of the Crown of France. And so she arrived in Paris at the age of fifteen to marry Louis le Jeune (Louis VII) bringing her superb inheritance, the Duchy of Aquitaine, Guyenne, Gascony, le Saintonge and le Poutou, the greatest wedding gift ever offered to the French Crown, vaster than the King's own little Île de France. She was the last representative of the House of Aquitaine.

Aliénor caused a stir in Paris. Looks it seems was only one of her attractions. A contemporary said she was more than beautiful. In today's language she would be called a trophy wife but trophies came with their own troubles, and these came to a head when she went on crusade with her husband. The thing was, men couldn't resist her charm, nor she theirs it seems, which upset things at the scrupulous court in Paris. According to the chronicles of the time the King adored her. The great influence on his life, however, was Bernard of Clairvaux, who believed pleasure had to be renounced and life lived in fear. Aliénor's arrival, from the pagan south, in a gust of exuberance, knocked over a few of these values.

The role of a medieval king was halfway to sainthood. He was God's representative, anointed by oils brought from heaven by a dove. He had the power to heal with his touch, so most kings put on a suitable show of piety. In Louis's case the show was unnecessary; he genuinely meant it and that was his problem. She complained that she was married to a monk, not a king.

Aliénor would become the wife of two and the mother of two kings and would be as powerful as any of them. She coincided with the age of Gothic. Gothic was light and flamboyant. It defied gravity; she too defied the gravity of a female in a male world. For fifteen years she was Queen of France, for thirty-five years, Queen of England, and after her father's death she was the equivalent of Queen of Aquitaine.

We left the Palais de Justice and headed towards our next site. On the way Treasa got an urge to go to the toilet. She went into a restaurant to ask if she could use theirs. She was waiting so long in a queue to ask permission that the urgency overcame her and she slipped in unnoticed, or so she thought, until she spotted a waitress following her down the street afterwards. The WC, the waitress explained, was for clients' use only.

"Sorry I hadn't realised that," explained Treasa in her best French.

But nothing much to be done about it now, I guess.

There was actually.

The waitress gave her a choice. Treasa could return to the restaurant and have a cup of coffee, which would satisfy the conditions of having to be a client, in a retrospective way. Or she could pay €1.50, the price of the use of the toilet for non-clients. Going back for coffee on her own seemed like a clumsy way out of the problem so she just paid the money. She said afterwards that it was, without contest, the costliest pee she had ever had.

In France they are mighty mean about letting non-clients use their facilities. It is understandable in a way. You can imagine that on market day, for example, when a mass of humanity from every corner of the locality descends on a town, shops and restaurants don't especially want to offload the gallons of urine produced over a full morning. Still, it sounds pretty ungenerous to be so fixed about refusing. I remember once asking in a flower shop in a small town if I could use their WC. The man said yes, but a sullen woman (I think she was his wife) said they had none. I presume she meant none for customers. For a few minutes I danced from foot to foot waiting to see which had the casting vote. Alas, she had. I felt like throwing the flowers I had bought at her. But I had paid for them by then, so I imagine she would have shrugged in indifference and sold them to someone else. I rushed into the garage next door. Yes, I was told, I could use theirs if I was going to buy petrol. The car was parked a quarter of a mile away. It would have been a roundabout way out of my problem to get the car and drive back to the garage, even if I could have held out that long. There's one thing about the French though – they are lenient towards people peeing in the open.

Anyway, we continued with our tour of Poitiers, on to the church of Saint Hilaire-Le-Grand. What made Saint Hilaire-Le-Grand grand was that he brought Christianity to this region in the fourth century. The story goes that Clovis, the founder of the French nation and its first Christian king, once camped near Poitiers. In the middle of the night he saw the cross of the basilica of Saint Hilaire light up and point out the position of the army of Visigoths. This was the clue that led Clovis to find these heretics. And thanks to the guiding light in this very basilica, he was able to rain fire on these non-believers and got the name Le Grand for his trouble. That would surely have advanced the cause of the true faith no end.

Today we don't go in for that kind of faith blasting. Tolerance is the new creed – tolerance for everyone bar the intolerant, which no doubt serves them right. It might teach them a bit of tolerance.

This church of Saint Hilaire was a stopping-point for pilgrims on their way to Santiago de Compostela, and they came to pray over the body of this great saint. But the crowds go to Puy – another church further south which also claims to have his remains – for the same reason. Dual claims to relics and bodies are not unusual.

The greatest feat of the next church we visited – dedicated to Saint Porchaire – was its existence. It narrowly escaped the hammers of the demolition workers when Poitiers City Council planned to widen the street in 1843, to make it more suitable for modern use. The campaigners launched into action to oppose it. We can be forever grateful to them; they not only saved the church but the medieval street too. Today narrow streets are one of the features that give Poitiers its medieval look. This church steps unpretentiously on to the pavement and fits unfussily between the houses and shops along the street. Saint Porchaire himself was a sixth-century hermit whose grave once attracted crowds of pilgrims. His relics are here, at least so they say, but we weren't going to start looking for proof. We lit a candle. It had become a habit, to light a candle in the churches we visited. Treasa said it had a nice feeling about it, that something stayed glowing on your behalf after you had left. Even Declan was keen about the candle idea, though it didn't fit in with the rest of his logic. It cost €1.50, the same as the use of the WC in the restaurant.

When I was buying a book on Poitiers' local history in the bookshop, I had to sift through a wide range of publications of France in bygone days, on village life long ago, La Vendée a hundred years ago, La Bourgogne in times gone by and a host of other books on the past. I don't know if the French are more wistful than the rest of us, or if they stoke it up more, but this kind of nostalgia is very evident, especially in bookshops.

The book I chose gave a general outline of the history of the town. At the cash desk I asked if they could recommend a restaurant for lunch. Two women agreed on the place next door. Two people's opinion could not be ignored, so minutes later we were seated on the terrace in a spot well shaded from the midday sun. I wanted a salad but the only suitable one on the menu had goat's cheese. Goat's cheese brings me out in a rash, not that I troubled the young waiter with that piece of information on my allergic woes; I just asked if they could leave out the cheese. And they did, though they left in the price. So many restaurants do that. It is as if the price is carved in stone or, more permanent still, programmed into a computer. If you asked for something extra I feel sure they would manage to uncarve the price somehow or unlock their computer code. Overall it was bad value, even before it rained.

We had nearly finished eating when a sudden shower of slanting rain sent clients seated at the outer edges fleeing for cover. It didn't reach us because we were under a canopy (two, as it turned out) so we continued our meal at our ease. We even felt smug in our luck to be so sheltered compared to the poor unfortunates scurrying indoors, leaving behind half-eaten meals, smouldering cigarettes and unfinished glasses of wine to be diluted by the rain. When the shower was over and the hot sun had dried everything almost instantly, clients resumed where they had left off. The rain soon was forgotten. Until, suddenly, as if out of nowhere, a heavy fall of water descended on to our table. For a minute it felt as if someone had upturned a bucket of water on us. Treasa got the heaviest soaking of all. She fled her chair as if it was burning and flailed around on the terrace. And she had good reason. Her hair normally stands frizzily out from her head but now it was sleeked wet. She looked like an animal who had taken a swim. You could have laughed but it would have been decidedly inadvisable to do so at that moment. The rest of us were wet too, but not that bad.

It took a few seconds to realise what had happened. Declan gave an explanation: the water had lodged in the folds of one of the parasols above us, and our table was placed underneath where two canopies came together. The overloaded water then crashed on us. His formulaic explanation made Treasa all the madder. And she told him sternly that she didn't care much what the reason was. She was more interested in drying herself.

What would they do for us, we asked? The two young waiters just shrugged and said it wasn't their mistake. Would they do nothing at all to dry us? But they just reshrugged. The French shrug must be the most all-embracing of disclaimers. It was not their fault, they repeated. We knew that. It was not their fault in the sense that they hadn't personally got water and spilt it over us. But what about a gesture of goodwill towards clients? A towel? A complimentary drink perhaps, or a reduction in the bill? But they stuck to their principles. Sure, rain is an act of God; no one was disputing that. But while it might be God's idea to send rain, it was hardly he who put two canopies together with a table underneath. At least if that's the way he does things I hate to think of what a botch he's making up there of heaven. We paid the bill – expensive even if we had never received a soaking – and as the waiter handed us the receipt, he wished us *Bonne Journée* (have a nice day), which sure sounded trying – enough to spoil a day, in fact – especially for Treasa. Have a good day, just don't expect us to contribute to making it good.

And so we set off to continue our tour of Poitiers, and the good wish, however meaningless, maybe helped to dry us off, though we probably owed more thanks to the hot sun for doing that.

I like how the renovation of this city is associated with the train. It was in 1869 that the City Council began its big town project, around the time of the arrival of the most modern form of transport. When you think of it, the train must have been one of the most life-changing of events. When the railway hacked and hewed its way across the landscape, life would never be the same again. Like the banshee's wail pre-empted death, the train's whistle announced the death of an old way of life. Horses could never level time and space like steam. And the train brought the capital to the provincial doorstep. No wonder they needed to do the place up. Renovated Poitiers got notions of Haussmann-style boulevards from Paris. The new town hall was built in a style that looked rather like the capital's Hôtel de Ville.

We had a quick look around the town hall but they were doing restoration work, so we were limited in what we could see. The stained glass window where Aliénor is represented granting the *charte de commune* (a charter giving Poitiers communal rights in 1199) was covered up with scaffolding. To declare a place a commune meant the population was no longer tied to an allegiance to the local lord.

If the train brought Paris to the provinces at a speed unknown until then, so too could it transport warring armies. Prussians troops crossed the Rhine in 1870 after Bismarck tricked Napoleon III of France into declaring war. Defeat knocked France off her perch as Europe's greatest power and that status passed on to the new united Germany. It was a humiliating moment in French history. For Poitiers, it delayed the renovation project, though it did get finished later.

We walked back towards the centre to take a look at the Church of Notre Dame La Grande. It's described as the town's signature landmark. And well it merits the title. It is not grand in size, indeed quite the opposite; it's neat and cosy. It glows with colour. Columns are painted in geometric designs, colour from top to bottom, not a square inch is left unpainted. Hardly any of the columns match, but, far from making the overall effect disjointed, it is warm and unifying. Red stands out most – red for happiness. Then yellow – the colour of jauntiness. Then blue – the hue of heaven. Columns circle around the altar and the wall rounds off behind it with decorative statues recessed at intervals. It's a place mixed with mystery and homeliness. When the shafts of midday sun came through the roof lights that day, as we looked towards the altar, it felt as if we were in a megalithic passage tomb receiving the rising sun. We stayed for a while and after we had finished our tour of Poitiers we came back to linger a little longer.

By accident we stumbled into Jasmin Citronnelle for an afternoon pick-me-up. It was certainly not the entrance – so narrow and unimpressive – that caught the eye. Once beyond the door, though, a bright and flowery space opened up, bearing the enchantment of a wonderland. On the brochure they describe it as a tearoom that is unlike the others. That's true. They say it is a *salon de thé,* outside of time, where you can capture the atmosphere of long ago, of having tea at your auntie's or your grandmother's. More French nostalgia, but true. It sounded like the reminiscent conversation we had indulged in ourselves over tea in Angers.

We had to wait a few minutes for a table. Treasa was really taken with the place. Her one regret however was that we hadn't discovered it before lunch. I was going to agree, because the salads being carried past us looked crunchy and bountiful. But before I could, Declan reminded her that she should be grateful for having found something good and not to be spoiling it by saying it was a pity it didn't happen earlier.

"Of course you weren't the one who got your hair wet, were you?" she said, rather missing his point about the futility of regret. It was funny because he has a limited amount of hair to get wet in any case. "In fact," she went on, " if I remember correctly you were the one who got the least rain, or the piled-up water, or whatever it was you called it."

Just at that moment, with superb timing, the waitress approached to tell us our table was ready. And soon, over a fine choice of teas, coffees and herbal teas, we were chatting as if nothing had happened. Not another reference was made to useless regrets, piled-up water, wet heads, lucky escapes or whatever. We were served in antique china, mismatching cups and plates. It was a place worthy of a long afternoon's chat. Four people at the table near us were doing just that, it seemed. The snatches of discussion that drifted our way sounded ever so scholarly – a philosophical debate, it seemed from the bits we could understand.

The menu offered a wide selection of salads, dishes for vegetarians and for those with unusual dietary needs: pastry for diabetics, dairy-free and gluten-free products. They hosted evenings of poetry readings, stories, traditional song, some in the local dialect. Very appropriate, in this the homeland of troubadour poetry. And they exhibited paintings, jewellery, photos, collages. It was a hub for thinkers, alternative thinkers, deep thinkers, free thinkers.

One proof of Poitiers' history of free-spiritedness is that it was here the terms *bourg* and *bourgeois* (burgess) first appeared, in 1016, in the cartulary. Today the word *bourg* means a small market town but in its original sense it was an area where the locals enjoyed freedom from the authority of the sovereign and *bourgs* grew up around the region. Guillaume the Troubadour granted some rights, like the freedom to young women and widows to marry without the permission of the lord. Quite a liberty, that, in the eleventh century, the equivalent today of letting your teenage daughter marry after a week's high-powered romance, I would say.

A university was founded here in 1431, during the brief period from 1418 to 1436 when Poitiers became the capital of France, while Paris was under English control. Later the place became a centre of Humanism. In Rabelais' book, *Gargantua,* frolicking university students had their meeting place around the great dolmen, where they had their rituals and festivals. This standing stone is still there, 6.7 metres long, 4.9 metres wide and 2.1 metres high. France's famous philosopher, Descartes, studied in the university here in Poitiers too and his ideas were to have a big future in France.

In today's ladder of French values, probably next to rustic life comes intellectual prowess. Modern secular France has held on to a lot of the literary education that they were so critical of in the late nineteenth century when the religious ran the schools. When the Prussians defeated them in war they believed that it was their technical-style schooling that helped them win, so they began fervently kicking the religious out of education. But France still prefers the literary to the technical. They're very impressed by the printed word and mastery of the French language. To write a book is a proud thing to do; it keeps alive a long tradition of scholarly pursuit. This is very evident in political life.

In most countries politicians write a memoir as a record of their political career; in France your book helps to launch your life in politics. Sarkozy, Ségolène Royal, Dominique de Villepin, Jospin, Pompidou, Mitterand, de Gaulle all have had books published. Clemenceau wrote an opera. This writing mania gets the political class accused of elitism, however.

Writing is not the only thing that has the whiff of elitism. French public life is controlled by an influential group: the graduates of the high and mighty École nationale d'administration (ENA). It was set up by de Gaulle for the brightest of civil servants and public figures. Politicians say they will put an end to this symbol of elitism, usually before elections, though afterwards, like a lot of pre-election burning issues, it cools off.

After afternoon tea there was just one site left to visit, the cathedral. The others were tired and had no great desire to go but I wanted to see the labyrinth which is said to have the same design as the one on the floor of Chartres Cathedral.

"If it's the same, what's the need to go and see it?" asked Steve.

But he was joking and in the end they all agreed.

The cathedral was disappointing. It was built a few feet below ground level and it had an underground feel to it. The labyrinth turned out to be hard to find. When we did finally locate it, on the wall on the north aisle, it was hardly surprising it took us so long. It looked trivial, like something a child would draw with chalk on a stone.

"So this is it?" said Steve, half laughing. It doesn't match all the trouble we took to find it."

Treasa and I agreed that it was pretty unimpressive. But Declan said that in fact its primitive look was its appeal, you could appreciate its antiquity all the more. And we did begin to see it differently.

"I wonder," asked Treasa, "how you'd perform the ritual they were doing on the labyrinth in Chartres?"

"You'd have to go up the wall," laughed Steve.

"You'd reflect on it mentally," suggested Declan, "not physically."

A lovely idea, the more you thought about it.

The stained glass window of the crucifixion behind the cathedral's altar was donated by Aliénor and her new husband, whom she married on 18 May 1152, just two months after her marriage to Louis VII of France was dissolved. There were a few difficulties with her marriage to Louis; high among them must have been his monk-like qualities. Her new husband, no monk he, was the nineteen-year-old Duke of Normandy, Count of Anjou and Maine, Henry Plantagenet and future Henry II of England.

The reaction at the court of France when she left was one of fury. The official reason given for the annulment was consanguinity. It was time they thought of it, they had two daughters by then. And that was part of the trouble, no male heir. The other problem was rumour had linked Aliénor with a number of men. The adultery of a queen was treason to the royal blood. Had Louis wanted, he could have had her burned to death and claimed Aquitaine. But he didn't and she took her duchy with her when she left him, and vassals of Louis who had been installed in castles in Aquitaine were replaced by Aliénor's.

Louis's loss was Henry's gain. Their combined empires – her Aquitaine, his Angevin – were put to work for the conquest of England and on 19 December 1154, at Westminster Abbey, they were crowned King and Queen of England, a kingdom stretching from the Scottish border to the Pyrénées. As if to add insult to injury to the King of France, the firstborn Plantagenet was male.

By the time we left the cathedral, evening was advancing and though I would have liked to have had one more look around, I knew better than to ask the others, who thought that the last visit was already a concession. And so we walked towards the centre where our car was parked. We had to shed the layers of history we had wrapped ourselves in for the day and head back to Brétignolles, by the A10 motorway, towards Niort and then the A83 by La Roche-sur-Yon and Aizenay.

We spent the next few days relaxing in Brétignolles before our next historic trip, to the Abbey of Fontevraud, where the bodies of Aliénor, Henry and their son, Richard the Lionheart, lie. The days were sunny, and we lazed on the beach and fought the mighty waves to have a swim. When the heat of day turned to evening we took brisk walks along by the seashore, coming to a halt only to view the lovely sunsets.

# CHAPTER 11

The grass had been cut in the low-lying meadows along by the Vendéen coast on the morning we left Brétignolles for Fontevraud Abbey. Rounds of harvested hay were enjoying the freedom of the fields in a carefree interlude between mowed meadow and winter feeding. As you passed by you could fancy feeling the blades of sharp stubble beneath your feet and smelling the pungent withered grass. Inland, towards Cholet, the landscape began to rise out of its flatness. Small fields reaching into high ground looked playful, like children gripping the crest of a hill with their hands, to have a peep at what was on the far side. Further in from the coast, land levels got more daring still. A great viaduct showed off its immense traversing power across a deep valley.

We drove on to the D960, a road that twists and meanders. Most sharp turns were taken care of by a roundabout. Part of this road is a three-lane nightmare. I think roads like these should be banned. If you overtake and the driver coming towards you decides to do the same, you have a single lane between the two of you and that can carry all the consequences your imagination has at its disposal. Steve was driving and he wanted to overtake, but we talked him out of it even though his patience was a little tried by the slow driver in front.

"It's more dangerous staying behind someone who's driving this slowly than overtaking," he said.

And we agreed that maybe so, but still we urged him not to.

It was a few minutes past ten o'clock as we approached the exit for the village of Vihiers, a little too early for morning coffee, but we figured that by the time we reached the next suitable town it might be too late, so we turned off.

Vihiers was a pleasant surprise of a place. We spotted a nice-looking tearoom, part of a boulangerie-pâtisserie. Clients waiting in the queue for service greeted us as if we were locals, bringing us into a close-knit world of village friendliness. The door to the tearoom at the back of the shop was blocked by a large cardboard box, a sign that few clients stopped there for tea. The slender woman came outside the counter to remove it and let us in. As we seated ourselves, Treasa wondered how she kept herself so slim with so many temptations around her. She concluded that there must be truth in the claim that French women never get fat in spite of their great love of food. It has been the subject of a book, *French Women Don't Get Fat*. So now women of other nationalities can read it and they too can defy the weighty law of logic. The author, Mireille Guiliano, has a cookbook to go with it, which, she says, is organised around her three favourite pastimes: breakfast, lunch and dinner.

The tearoom wouldn't really have accommodated many more than the four of us. The woman strode in from the shop to ask us if it was all right to serve some other customers before looking after us. We agreed. We were in no hurry at all, so it would have been a shame to deprive French clients of their fresh morning bread. And so she served the stream of people who came through the open door, stepping on the doormat, which rang a bell as they entered (it rang again when they were leaving making business sound doubly brisk). The ritual was the same for each client: the *bonjour*, taking the order, serving, the payment, the thanks and the *bonne journée* wish. Not a single one of these essentials was omitted for any client, despite the great number. Equal hospitality for all. And it rang out like a song. But, more than likely, only we heard it that way. Unblunted by the hypnosis of habit, it went straight to our third ear, with all its notes and unfamiliar resonances.

When finally there was a break in the stream, she asked us what we would like. Treasa ordered: croissants and coffee for four.

Sorry, there were no croissants.

"Well, in that case, coffee and a slice of baguette, then, perhaps."

That was possible all right but there was no butter.

"Well, just jam is fine then."

There was no jam either.

We persevered. We settled for coffee and brioche with nothing on it. Even after all those difficulties – no jam, no butter, no croissant – it was a strangely thrilling experience. We took a walk around the village before leaving which, in such a small place, only took minutes.

After leaving Vihiers we went on the D748 passing by the villages of Trémont, Concurson-sur Layon, Doué-La-Fontaine. This is Loire heaven. Sunflower fields curved their yellow heads in circles within circles, like a throng of friendly children waving us on our way. The ever faithful rows of trees, that the French are so fond of, ruled off in the distance. We branched off into the very narrow D205 to Fontevraud, but it was so small we decided to turn back, against the pushy advice of the sat nav, and we went through Saumur instead. It's longer but worth the extra distance, we all reckoned, even Treasa, whose resistance to the temptation of a narrow road is weakest. Pleasant and all as byroads are, if they're so slender that you're afraid you will be edged off by oncoming traffic, then the worry is greater than the enjoyment.

The Romanesque Abbey of Fontevraud is three miles south of where the River Vienne meets the Loire. It holds the tomb of Aliénor, Henry II of England and their son Richard the Lionheart. It is all that is left of the great Angevin Empire, its final chapter. I was expecting it to be a ruin but it is very much a living place. Its site, in a hollow, doesn't weigh it down with the same underground feeling that the cathedral in Poitiers suffers from. In fact, the high countryside that rises above it into dense woodland encloses it in a pleasant shelter, a gentle resting place. The effigies of the Queen and Kings are there. Their colour is somewhat faded, as you would expect, but in good shape considering the passing of time. Aliénor is reading a book, which is fitting for this great patron of poets. They say it's a Bible. She wasn't pious in real life. She had, of course, no say in the decision to present her as prayerful in death.

The place is ornate. It bears the noble fingerprints of royal patronage. Dormitories, refectories, nuns' embroidery room and a chapter house surround a courtyard that's lit up with some stained glass beauties. Sixteenth-century murals of the passion of Christ and some portraits of former abbesses hang on the walls. One of the reception areas was ready for a wedding. Flowers and chairs tied up with chiffon bows were waiting to receive the couple and their guests.

"This is one more wedding album for us to spoil," said Steve.

This time we didn't. We left before the wedding party arrived.

The British and the French have long fought over this piece of burial ground in Fontevraud. The British government thought their favourite kings should be buried in their "own" country. The funny thing is that all three of them were much more French than English. But what do facts matter?

It was in England rather than France that Richard, the striking six-footer with the red golden hair, reached hero status. That was in spite of the fact that he squeezed his English dominions until the pips squeaked, gathering money first for his Crusade, then for his ransom and finally for his wars with King Philip Augustus of France. To win back Angevin territory he sold everything. He said he would have hocked the city of London if he could have found a buyer. And still the English showered him with love. They made up stories of his friendship with Robin Hood. To explain his nickname, Lionheart, they claimed he had wrestled with a lion and tore out its heart.

In Queen Victoria's time discussions about bringing these royals "home" reached an advanced stage, and France had agreed to transfer the bodies. But then war broke out with Prussia in 1870 and that gave the French more to worry about than trying to satisfy British emotions about "their" hero kings. The plans were dropped and no mention that I know of has been made in recent years. Steve said that these kind of claims just might bring up awkward questions of restitution and before you'd know it the Elgin Marbles might be up for discussion, or Mona Lisa and her companions might be on their merry way to Italy, and who knows where it would all end?

The village of Fontevraud is very geared towards tourists, with plenty of inviting places to eat. There are a few quaint buildings. Declan pointed out a comically shaped one. It came to an acute angle, which must have made the interior look a little odd. It was obviously built to fit into an allocated space and the obstruction had long since disappeared. They hadn't yet acquired the fondness of the modern age for knocking down anything that stood in their path. Steve said it had the appearance of a place where, if a manure heap stood in the way, they would have built around it rather than move it.

We had lunch nearby, and though there were only ourselves and another four in the restaurant, the waiter was about to serve us what the others had ordered. I would hate to see what mix-up there might have been if the large number of tables had been full. When our plates arrived, Declan said he regretted not having accepted the first offering because they looked a whole lot nicer.

We made our way back towards Saumur by France's great hunting ground. These thick forests, full of game and wild with pleasure, once filled the idle days of the gentry. Good horsemanship, wrestling with danger, the nerve to inflict pain were all part of the life of the gentleman. Hunting is an old rural tradition and the French have stuck with it, though it is no longer the preserve of an elite group. More people are licensed to hunt in France than in any other European country, and they enjoy a longer season. Hunting, *la chasse*, was one of the gains of the French Revolution and they guard it vigilantly. They're a powerful lobby group and they take exception when soft-hearted urban dwellers grumble about cruelty to animals. No politician – except maybe Green spoilsports – would be foolish enough to kill the joy of the French *chasseurs*.

Steve thinks there's a world of difference between pursuing animals for sport and killing to feed your family.

But Treasa makes no distinction. "Killing is killing and there's no need for it. The thing is you can live quite well without meat. A large proportion of the world does. So there's no argument about it," she said.

The answer is not so clear-cut in my own head, but I don't like meat so I don't have to make any decision about the rights or wrongs of it.

Declan has no qualms. "If we didn't kill animals they'd kill us," he said.

"Now at last we know that these stories they were so fond of in the Middle Ages about wrestling with bears and pulling out the hearts of lions had their uses after all. They were just getting ahead before they killed them," said Steve.

Declan went on to explain his guiltlessness: "Everything we do in this life is at someone else's expense and that's the way it works. Every step we take kills some insect or other. Even if you take an antibiotic you kill the bacteria."

"That's entirely different," said Treasa.

But Declan was having none of it. "No. We do things to suit ourselves. Even when we feed the birds we put it on a bird-table where the magpies and the pigeons can't get at it, just because they're not as pretty as the smaller birds. We're just a superficial species. And people have a lot less of a problem eating fish just because fish aren't as cuddly as lambs or calves. You couldn't imagine having a pet fish."

"I could," said Steve. "We always had goldfish when I was young."

Just then a car came speeding around the corner, well out from his (and it was a he) own side of the road, which brought our discussion to a rapid close. And so the question of whether to be or not to be a vegetarian remained unsolved.

In the village of Champigny a lively market was going on. It is always tempting to stop because French markets look such colourful affairs. But, the following day, Sunday, was market day in Brétignolles and this one in Champigny looked very minor compared to it.

Next morning, in our enthusiasm, we arrived too early. Some

of the vendors were only setting up their stalls. The market centres on Brétignolles' church square and it trails along the streets that fan out from the intersection, along by the back of the cemetery wall and up the length of the street that leads to the floral roundabout in front of the town hall and along by the library and community centre.

Food occupies the central space on the square – sausages, salami, pickles and cheeses of all kinds. This is France after all, where there are as many cheeses as days in the year. De Gaulle only counted 246 of them when he asked how he could rule a country with all those cheeses.

The thing about French markets is that they're a lot more than a buying and selling event. Ritual and tradition are woven in there too. The local market has traces of carnival, of theatre, of a fair day, a fun day, a family day out. The quietness of the supermarket on market day shows the definite preference the French have for food bought in the open air.

Shop doors were flung open along the street to benefit from the custom of the passers-by, breaking all the French rules on Sunday working. It only takes a glance to make out locals from tourists. Holidaymakers dawdle at every colourful stall, to view jewellery, to pick up florid beach wear, or to try on broad-rimmed hats and other useless wares. But the locals move with a business-like spring in their step. That morning they buzzed around the food stalls carrying large wicker baskets. Dogs stuck their little heads out of some of them. I expect they had to walk the journey home when the baskets filled with supplies for the week. Apart from putting these dirty little mutts into a basket that's used for food, I can't understand why French dogs have such a problem with walking like dogs of every other nationality.

I'm sure the locals no longer heard the cries of the vendors as they showed off the many uses their pots, pans, vegetable graters, knives or other kitchen implements could be put to, because repeated words get lulled by their own repetition. But for tourists, the voices came in their raw purity. That morning they mingled with the ringing of the church bells. Worshippers swelled the crowds as they poured out of the beige, Spanish-looking church after Mass ended. The low average of worship in France must be brought up considerably by the big attendance in Catholic Vendée. Even the *curé* (parish priest) joined in the event that day. He was seated at a table outside the church, selling his book of poetry.

We strolled along the road by the library, by the stand where we had bought belts the previous Sunday. Noon was approaching and as the sun beat down without mercy, the strong smell of leather hung in the air. We nodded to the sun-tanned man who was surrounded by leather goods of all description. He recognised us from the previous market day. We had no custom for him. We had bought ourselves all the belts we needed the week before, as well as belts for all our friends, so many that he offered us a free gift.

I spotted a dress I fancied. I wondered was there any way of trying it on. The man at the stand suggested, with a roguish smile, the back of a van. And just as I was about to pull it over my head, the back door of the vehicle creaked open. I grabbed it shut and the salesman and another few fellows nearby began laughing helplessly. Not the best sales tactics but a change from the political correctness that has taken over these days. I didn't buy but at least he got a good laugh.

We strolled past stands strewn with tablecloths, curtains, bedcovers and fabric of every hue. They were draped over their allotted areas and escaped from underneath their canopies to lie fully exposed in the hot sun. There were racks with heavy clothing for sale too. It was hard to imagine on such a hot day that you might ever need such warm clothing, even though you had gone through enough seasons to know that winter would follow. That day all you could consider were the piercing rays of sunlight, drawing shapes and shadows and unleashing a mood of light and lightheartedness that made you smile.

The church in Brétignolles was hosting a concert that evening. We didn't want to miss it though it wasn't the most suitable time for an outing because we had to clean the place we had been renting before leaving early next morning. There's a funny tradition with rented accommodation: you have to clean up after you. Wouldn't it be strange if they asked you to clean a hotel room before you left?

As the bell rang out the evening hour, we walked up the steps of the church. Right through day and night this bell keeps watch, chiming out the quarter hour, whether or not anyone is listening. The church meshes with the buildings around it, though it's a lot older than most of them. They're all painted in a pastel shade that soaks up the bright sunlight with ease. As Declan turned the old handle of the church door and pushed it open creakily, the sound of plucked strings and tuning instruments floated in our direction. The place pulsed with a sense of anticipation. Church concerts have a buzz about them that you don't get in a theatre or concert hall. I think it's the "making do" effect that gives them this special atmosphere. People make a extra effort to get over the problems of a place being put to use for something beyond its normal function. Some had brought along cushions to soften the hardness of the church pews.

The musicians were already on the altar "stage". They launched into a music that was light and dancey – Strauss's polkas, American marches, waltzes. It rounded off our stay in Brétignolles with a flourish. We had intended leaving before the show ended, to get on with the cleaning, but as we got caught up in the atmosphere, we changed our minds and our shared glances showed we were all at one in putting off the cleaning until the morrow. It was not a decision we would relish early next morning but we could worry about that later.

# CHAPTER 12

Next morning, cleaning, polishing and shining complete, we were on our way northwards, in the direction of home, though we still had some places to visit.

There's something about driving along the open road, moving with the landscape – all your belongings with you – that makes the nomad in you delight. Far into the distance an approaching hillock showed its flank, light glittering on its gentle slope, which made me reminisce about home. I'm sure it was someone's earliest horizon, someone's sacred hill, but we passed swiftly by.

We came by Cholet then northwards, on to Loire country on a network of D roads and finally to the D751, the closest road to the river's southern banks, driving against the flow of the water. From this side you wouldn't think the Loire was the home of Renaissance vanity and high-flying conceit. As we rose up and descended, at times circling corkscrew style, we caught odd glimpses of the river, but for most of the journey you couldn't see water at all. This must be one of the nicest roads in France but it was quiet that day. The few cars we met weren't speeding. Just as well because the road was narrow. We met tractors, sprinklers, the mail van. It was ever so homely. You might as well have been in the remotest of regions for all life's rush had found its way in. If you had opened the car window you would quite likely have heard the water's flow, or a dog's bark, or a cock crowing. France is the most visited country in the world, and this is one of the most popular tourist regions in France. Where were they all that day? Why did they leave this piece of heaven all to us?

Tillage fields passed by, pages of them, drills of market gardening, of high value crops, broken from time to time with small clumps of trees. This is vine country. The vine has been harvested around here for centuries. It is not a demanding plant. It does not ask for rich soil but it does need warmth. So, this far north, it needs a sheltered spot, well shielded from cold breezes, where all the available sun can be trapped. Plants looked uniform, like a guideline in a handwriting exercise book. The more tender ones were protected – from the birds, I presume – in poly tunnels of white and green. The volley of sprinklers sometimes missed their target and we got a free car wash – no bad thing – but the driver had to be alert and have windscreen wipers at the ready, in case his vision turned liquid.

Lots of signs pointed to châteaux. They were really big houses with turrets, châteaux in terms of wine production, not the classic châteaux of the Loire Valley. Signs welcomed us to Muscadet country. If you were to take up all the invites to taste the local produce – *la dégustation* – you'd be three sheets in the wind, your car in the river.

The delight of the fleeting morning made me muse how lovely it would be to live here, to make permanent this passing pleasure. But, on second thoughts, no. Fleeting delight is delightful only because it's fleeting. You can wish all you like to make it permanent but I bet if you did, if you moved here, the weight of the daily grind would find out where you were and follow you, and you would soon find yourself worrying about the things that get to you at home and make you look forward to holidays: paying the bills, cleaning down the cobwebs, getting the children to do a bit of study. No. Joy is joy only if savoured in short teasing tastes – *la dégustation* – just to tell you how great life can be, but isn't all the time.

We stopped in Champtoceaux, the first fairly substantial place where coffee might be available. It is on a hill and that morning it oozed all the charm of the French village: flowery, unpretentious, quietly taking life easy. We walked to the top of the hill. The day was heating up, preparing itself for some high temperatures later. They were expecting a wedding in the honey-coloured church on the hilltop. Doors were open heavily and highly, flowers, music, all ready to burst into joy. As we drank coffee in the green-framed glass veranda of the hotel beside the church, the chic guests began to arrive: men in black formal wear, women holding on to their hats in case the breeze swiped them off their heads and into the valley beneath. This time we were safely in the hotel, well out of the reach of cameras.

After Champtoceaux, the road descended to the level of the water, in a semi-corkscrew fall. Views of the north side of the river, some with châteaux, jumped in and out of view, as if her ladyship was tempting us to savour the far side of her banks.

A row of tiny villages along the D751 – la Rabottiere, le Marillais, Notre Dame le Marillais, Saint Florent-le-Vieil – have huge churches, some with rose windows. Their small population could hardly have justified this size of worship.

"Where did the money come from for such grandeur?" Declan wondered.

"Probably wine."

They must have been selling copious amounts of it to construct such fine buildings.

Mûrs Erigné is a small village close to Angers. We were aiming to be there for lunch, and all went beautifully to plan, except when we got there the place where we had hoped to eat was no longer there. We thought the summer foliage had obscured the sign, so we stopped to ask a woman who was walking her white terrier along the roadside.

"It's closed," she told us.

What a pity. It took us a few minutes to rearrange ourselves. You find so many things to miss about a place when it's gone. We had eaten in this small family restaurant the last time we were here. What made it nice was the cuisine, the fresh produce, the friendliness.

The woman with the terrier recommended a good replacement. It wasn't a place we would have gone with any great hopes, or indeed would have gone to at all without a recommendation. Local knowledge cannot be beaten. The restaurant was big, rectangular, pub-like, with leatherette chairs, a world away from the cosy family restaurant we had been looking for. They called themselves a *restaurant panoramique* and this was no false claim. It had a full length wall of window, overlooking the River Louet and the valley of the Loire.

The food was worthy of its reputation. We had large plates of salad decorated with sweet red grapefruit. I didn't want cheese in mine so they added other things to make up the loss. This is unusual generosity. We didn't delay over the meal, no time for after-lunch relaxing or idle chat. Our next stop was Angers, at one time the centre of a great empire, and we wanted to have a look around.

"We can go to a *salon de thé* in Angers and have tea and cakes. Or coffee. Or chocolat chaud. I just love… " Treasa was launching into one of the reveries she usually finds herself in when she talks about food.

"Yes, but we've to get there first," said Declan.

"Well, naturally," she answered curtly.

"Wouldn't that be some feat, to have coffee in Angers before we even got there?" said Steve.

We stopped briefly at Les Ponts-de-Cé. What is striking about this place is that it consists of one extended street about two miles long, with seven bridges. It crosses the Authion, the Louet, a canal and four other offshoots of the River Loire. I read that this important crossing has been the scene of military battles in practically every war from Caesar's to the Liberation in 1944. We took a photograph of the bridge, not of ourselves – we looked too grumpy. Early afternoon irritability had set in. It looked as if we too were shaping up for a battle, to add to the statistics of this town. We went for a short walk. Bad form eases with a walk. The footwork grounds it, I believe. I wonder what becomes of it then? Maybe it goes down into the underworld and waits there for the wicked after death. The wicked are those who cause arguments on holidays.

# CHAPTER 13

If a trip to France offered no more than a visit to a *salon de thé*, it would be worth it for that alone. The French infuse their tearooms with the sweetness of the idyllic. They do vary though, so it's worth searching for the best.

The men weren't fussy about where we went. "Isn't one tearoom the same as another?" said Declan.

How do you even go about answering someone like that?

They both looked embarrassed when Treasa said she'd ask a passer-by to recommend one.

"There's no need," urged Declan.

But she had already approached an oldish woman in flowery blue. She explained that she wanted a *pâtisserie* with a *salon de thé* attached. What she loves – and so do I – is to go to the counter and pick from the wide variety of cakes and pastries. It's a lovely yielding to temptation to choose from those miniature sculptures kept tenderly underneath glass casing, guarded like illuminated manuscripts.

The men kept their distance, looking down at the pavement, shuffling on their feet, saying nothing, but they looked as if there was plenty they could say. The woman gave the names of two places, placing the map on the car bonnet and painstakingly pointing out exactly where to go. But after having walked for ages to reach them, they turned out, both of them, to be shops that sold *pâtisserie* but had no *salon de thé* attached. There must have been some confusion somewhere. Either her question or else her understanding of the answer were wrong. Maybe both. Sometimes you phrase your question in perfectly written French but no one can grasp a word of what you say. I was thinking of quoting Mark Twain: "In Paris they simply stared when I spoke to them in French. I never did succeed in making those idiots understand their language."

Anyway, I thought it better to keep that citation to myself. Maybe later it could be laughed at. Bad humour is only funny when seen from afar. By the time we reached the second wrong destination a certain kind of silent atmosphere was building up, a holiday-type absence of words. Undoubtedly, Declan was thinking of the day he was blamed for not filling the petrol tank.

Third time lucky. The young woman we stopped knew exactly what we were looking for. "It's quite a long walk but it's worth it," she said with a knowing nod. "About twenty minutes. I'll walk you there. I'm going that way anyway." (I had the feeling she wasn't but the French find no effort too great to guide you towards good food.)

When our destination failed to turn up exactly at the end of the promised twenty minutes, the men began to go quiet again. It took us thirty-five minutes, in hot afternoon sun. It better be good, I prayed. It was hard to convince the men that we needed to walk so far when they were such Philistines as to think that one *salon de thé* was the same as another. Maybe Treasa was right about them both being colour blind. They might be "taste blind" as well.

She was right, the woman. It was worth the walk. The perfume of *pâtisserie* came floating through the open door. She had brought us to a place where the *pâtisserie* was finer than normal, and that's saying something in a country with a towering standard of confectionary. The menu read, *Nos entremets, nos tartes, nos gourmandises,...* The less you understood the more you fell under its spell. It also noted the house's ranking among France's hundred best *chocolateries*. I had a *mille feuille* (a thousand leaves). What a name. What lace-like intricacies it brings to mind. I went back for a second one – two thousand leaves.

All earlier disagreeableness had dissipated into a wonderful moment, a meshing of pure satisfaction. Touchiness is brought out more sharply on holidays. What bothers Declan is when someone in the group makes a wildcat decision to go somewhere that wasn't part of the plan. The offender is usually Treasa because what annoys her are rigid arrangements, when she can't let things flow, go wherever the day takes her. What gets to me is when I forget something, like a camera, and I spend the day brooding over the procession of wonderful sights I could have made permanent if only I had remembered. Steve is never too pushed one way or another, except to keep out of the way of insects. That day in the tearoom nothing was spoiled for any of us, all our good energies fused into one.

We fell into reminiscences. My childhood trips to a tearoom with my mother flooded back to me: the white linen tablecloth, starched solid, I could nearly feel grazing against my knee, cakes on a doily-decorated plate held high by the aproned waitress, the heartbeat of the waiting moment. My mother used to bend the rules. Not a word would she utter about spoiling my appetite or any of those droning rules of childhood. And she used to pretend not to see my stretching hand, often on its third journey to the plate.

It was her grandmother who used to bring Treasa for tea. She nearly burst into hymn recalling the beige corrugated paper cup that held the trifle cake in place. Then there was the sponge cake iced in pink from which she used to peel off the icing chunk by chunk, before launching into the spongy part, slowing down as she saw it coming to an end so as to savour it an instant longer.

Declan, not normally a man to reminisce, told us about the upstairs tearoom above the bakery where his father used to take him and his brother. His father never took any cakes himself; he would just read the newspaper and sip coffee. Then suddenly he'd pull the paper to one side and say: "My goodness, have you eaten all those? There was enough there for an army." No matter how many times he brought them he would say the same thing, and with equal surprise.

Steve had no memories at all of being brought for tea and he didn't understand what we were all so dreamy about. Being taken out on the boat with his father though, now that was a different thing entirely. He leaned forward on the table and his face took on a far-off look, as if he was ready for a long story.

Declan looked at his watch and suddenly the magic flow of memories got interrupted. We couldn't believe how time had passed. So we all agreed that really we could not afford to recall any more memorable moments. Much of the day was gone already. Some other time maybe we could hear all about Steve's outings on the boat. We had a lot of places to see. This was once a very important city.

So, to get on with the work of the day we had to turn our minds back to the twelfth century, when Angers was the centre of the Angevin Empire with Henry Plantagenet – the groom we had met in the cathedral in Poitiers and whose effigy we saw in Fontevraud – at its head. They were vassals of the King of France though they were far enough away from Paris to enjoy a lot of independence from his authority. The Angevin Empire was well placed to act as a buffer between Celt and Gaul.

Because the Angevins lacked a royal seal of origin they had to invent a tale to make them worthy of the awe that matched their power. And so it was said that the House of Anjou, though not royal, could trace a source more terrifying than most kings. They were descendents of Mésuline, the daughter of Satan. The story went that the earliest Count of Anjou, Fulk the Black, a terrifying individual, it seems, once did a trip and brought back a wife whose looks went beyond human beauty. She seldom attended Mass and when she did she left before the consecration. A dead giveaway, that. Because, did not everyone know that no devil could look the consecrated body and blood of Christ in the eye?

Cathedrals had their own tall stories to tell. In the great period of relic rivalry Angers and Amiens cathedrals both claimed to be the custodians of the head of John the Baptist. "A head-to-head contest," Steve called it. "Which of them had the genuine article I wonder? Which of them had the head that was presented to Salome on the plate?" he asked mischievously.

It reminded me of a story I heard of a holy man who visited a church where they showed him their proud possession: the head of Saint Anne. He said he thought he had already seen her head in another church and that it was somewhat smaller. "Ah yes," they explained, "that was the head of Saint Anne as a young woman."

We climbed the steps of the cathedral. At the entrance a suntanned man was dragging out a melancholy air on an accordion, humouring the instrument gently, coaxing it into soft tones. We could still hear it from inside the great doors as we viewed the Angers tapestries, which hung in a row along the wall. We didn't have time to investigate the head of John the Baptist. On our way out Treasa gave the accordion man a euro. She said she gives the equivalent of the enjoyment she gets. He began to play faster as we went down the steps. Steve reckoned he must have got a rush of energy from the euro.

We headed for the *train touristique* which circles the town centre. It saves a lot of footwork, but when we enquired in the tourist office they told us it was out of service that day because the driver was ill. The story had a personal feel to it, a lot nicer than to hear a computer had broken down. But it meant we had to get walking. We wandered around by the château, by stone mansions that dated from far in the past, by interesting wooden houses, but it was all too hasty and directionless.

We had to get to Chinon by evening which meant rushing away. It was all the reminiscing that we had indulged in over tea that had left us short of time. But to reminisce is as important as to study a town's history.

"It certainly is," Declan agreed "but you could do that at home."

True. So all further reminiscing was postponed until after our holiday.

# CHAPTER 14

The road from Angers to Chinon brought us across to the south of the River Loire at Saumur and on to the D749 for the final part of the journey. This route cuts through the traditional province of Touraine, the "garden of France" – a gentle landscape, a region of rivers. Three of the Loire's tributaries, the Cher, the Indre and the Vienne, flow through Tourraine. And three famous Frenchmen grew up in this region: Descartes, Rabelais and Balzac.

It was raining when we arrived in Chinon, so our planned walk around the town had to wait until next morning when we got up extra early to view the place. We climbed the steep hill, all ready to look at the castle. From this height you can view beneath you the row of fifteenth and sixteenth century houses along the narrow street that's sandwiched between the Plantagenet castle ruins on the hilltop and the River Vienne.

Alas, the castle was shut for renovations. From underneath the wrapping of netting and scaffolding you could hear the faint sounds of the hammers of restoration. So many places we wanted to see were undergoing renovation work that Steve reckoned that when they saw us coming, they rushed out and erected scaffolding and threw some safety netting up.

We paused for a few minutes, and then decided there was nothing for it but to go for coffee in one of the many cafés that lined the street on the town's lower level. It was a little early so we had to wait to be served. They were still arranging tables and fastening clips on tablecloths to stop them flapping in the breeze. The castle was visible from the terrace where we sat disappointed at having our plan foiled. Disappointment is a theme around here. Henry Plantagenet died here, in the castle we wanted to visit, in a serious state of disappointment – broken hearted, hated, humbled and deserted by his family.

I'm sure when Henry and Aliénor took their vows in the cathedral in Poitiers they had hoped for a happier ending than they got. Around the time their youngest child, John, was born things began to go downhill. Henry fell in love with Rosamund de Clifford (Fair Rosamund) and from then on Aliénor spent more time holding court in Poitiers, the land of her birth. She took up the role of her grandfather, the Duke Troubadour, as patron of poets, presiding over the Court of Love.

Courtly love, for all its mystical poetry, had a practical side to it. It was as much about a code of behaviour as a literary movement. It was about the art of love, of taste, of delicacy. Part of its purpose was to refine the court and transform sexual desire from an unchecked animal urge into something with a touch of the spiritual.

Because courtly love placed the woman at the centre of its focus, inevitably Aliénor became the subject of troubadour poetic reverence. Her patronage of poets had never been encouraged by either of her husbands (troubadours singing the praises of wives were potential seducers), not even Henry who was fond of a fling himself.

"Very typical," commented Treasa.

Henry had more and more to contend with towards the end of his life: problems with his family, the row over Becket's murder. A cult of Becket gained ground. In the wave of emotion that followed his death, the current of opinion saw him as a martyr for the cause of freedom from state tyranny, which had little to do with the facts. But what chance have facts against an upswell of sentiment?

Henry got more blame than he deserved. Whatever his faults, he was a fair ruler, taking fairness to the point of going against the popular grain. He imposed order without fear or favour, bringing England out of semi-barbarism. And he refused to join in the persecution of Jews or Albigensians, a popular trend of the time. For the death of Becket, Henry's domains were placed under interdict by the Pope. That amounted to a public show of the wrath of God. All religious life ceased, churches were locked up, bells silenced. Apart from baptism and absolution there were no sacraments: no ordinations, Masses, marriages, funerals. At the same time the spot where Becket was martyred became the scene of miracles.

But it was not his quarrel with the Pope or Becket that brought Henry down in the end but his rows with his sons. Aliénor encouraged them against him. Her former husband, Louis, also took sides against Henry. Whether he got any belated satisfaction from taking a swipe at his former rival I don't know. Henry forgave his sons but not Aliénor. He had her locked in prison for sixteen years.

Treasa said she would have done exactly the same in a similar situation.

"What? Locked her up?" Declan asked.

"No, encouraged children against a fickle husband."

Steve and Declan joked that they too would do the same as he did: lock her up.

Louis's son, Philip Augustus became King of France in 1180. This was Philippe le Dieu-Donné (the God-Given), the heir for whom Louis had to wait until his third marriage. He was the baby for whom the city of Paris burst into joy, went ablaze with bonfires and resounded with the ringing of bells. When he grew up he grabbed his chance to destroy the last of the Plantagenets and their in-fighting gave him his opportunity. By 1204 he had driven the English out of Normandy. Henry's son, Richard the Lionheart, joined Philip Augustus and imposed humiliating peace terms on his father at Chinon. Henry's final blow was when John, his youngest, joined the others against him. John was his favourite. (He must have been on his own in his love for John because history hasn't one good word to say about him.) Henry died in Chinon, aged fifty-six on 6 July 1189, worn out by action and grief. Even his servants stripped his dead body of the ceremonious clothing in which he had been laid out in the chapel at Chinon Castle. It was the only way they could recoup something of what they were owed, because their chances of ever getting payment from the victors were slim. The few who remained faithful found a crown, sceptre and ring, probably nicked from the statue of some saint or other, to send him on his way with a small semblance of royalty.

Steve reckoned that his humbling must have been the satanic Mésuline playing her final trick on the family. His body was carried from Chinon to Fontevraud for burial. Later Richard would join him in his burial spot at the young age of forty-two, and later still the eighty-two-year old Aliénor, who outlived both of them.

Steve complained of suffering from Plantagenet overdose. He wanted to sample the lighter side of Chinon and go to see the birthplace of François Rabelais, France's comic hero. Probably no one brings to life the French spirit as well as Rabelais does. The mere mention of his name is enough to raise a laugh among French people. Steve admires his way of turning life's serious things into fun. Treasa claims you become like the person you admire and certainly that would fit Steve's light attitude towards life.

So we headed for the Rabelais country home, La Devinière, about five kilometres west of Chinon. It was here the family grew their fresh produce and in autumn harvested their wine. Rabelais made a short visit to La Devinière in 1532, when he was in his late thirties (the date of his birth isn't certain; the most quoted one is 1494) and in the warm flush of nostalgia, the memories of his youth flooded back to him and gave him the flash of insight that set his pen flowing.

And flow it did. His stories of giants – Gargantua and Pantagruel – are charged with childhood frolics, part recollection, part legend. These giants had a huge capacity for eating and drinking. They cared little for authority. They roamed the fields and villages of these parts, playing pranks and speaking the dialect of the locals. They liked wine, camaraderie, adventure, women. They waged war although the massacres were so far-fetched that they could be placed safely beyond reality. The violence, the drunkenness, the obscenity, the coarseness are all diffused by their comic cover.

We drove in by the narrow winding roads leading to the house.

The place was dense with thick summer leaf. Like his writing, it had a warm abundance about it. It was nice to view the horizons he saw as a child, before his life's boundaries hardened into those of a grown-up. Admittedly, it would be stretching it to think the view hadn't changed since the sixteenth century but in a way it hasn't. The place is still rustic; no modern development is within view. And you see, more or less, the landscape that weaves through his writings – the pastures around Chinon and the River Vienne.

La Devinière is a museum now. It's an ordinary fifteenth century country house, built in stone with an outside staircase. It has a dovecot, which is not of great interest because it was added after Rabelais' time, but it is interesting for what it represents. The number of doves indicated the size of a landlord's property: one dove for every half hectare of land. Here there are enough for 288 doves. Doves caused great irritation. They might have shown off the extent of a landlord's possessions but they ate the peasants' crops and that became one of the contentious issues of the Revolution.

Behind Rabelais' fun and pranks a serious message lurks, a concern about what he saw around him. And there was a lot to be concerned about in Reformation France. In the guise of a buffoon, he takes authority down a peg by making fun of kings, popes, scholars, theologians, church abuses, legal abuses, hypocrisy and ignorance.

We got the full attention of the staff because there were so few there at the time. As we walked around La Devinière Steve talked about Calvin, who was a contemporary of Rabelais, and his different approach towards life. Steve has a special interest in Calvin because he's of Huguenot origin himself.

"Calvin really was a killjoy," he said. "His God didn't believe in giving people a sporting chance. Fancy a God who had already made up his mind that some would make it into heaven and others wouldn't, even before they took their first breath. I wonder if my ancestors took the same delight in gloom and doom as Calvin did?" he asked. "Give me Rabelais any day."

"If they did, you certainly don't seem to be infected by it," said

Treasa. Then she suggested: "There's a serious message in Rabelais' fun. Maybe there was a light message in Calvin's seriousness."

"If there is, it's well hidden," said Steve.

Rabelais saw life through comic eyes. He brought out the joy of food and wine, the juvenile fun of tricks and hoaxes. But most of all, his writings bring out the warmth of the earth and the French still hold on to that love of country life… and juvenile fun.

Perhaps it's because France industrialised late that country living and family farming casts such a spell over them. Painters, writers, politicians, restaurateurs and ordinary folk like to draw on the memory of being a people of the soil. It fits in with their gastronomy, buzzing markets, their unhurried existence and that strange term that they call, *la France profonde.*

*La France profonde* roughly translates as… Ah who cares what it means in another language? To translate is crude when it's a feeling, not an understanding, you're talking about. *France profonde* captures images of a liking for the old ways, of rolling hills and charming villages, of pungent earth and the joy of making it flourish.

I hate to interrupt the idyllic flow but *la France profonde* is mostly a myth. These days French farming is less and less like that of a time gone by. It is true that over half the country is in farmland, and that it is the European Union's biggest producer but only a tiny minority is involved in farming compared to, say, half a century ago when it employed about one third of French workers. And the small numbers who are, are mostly engaged in large-scale industrial-style exploitation of the land. Fewer and fewer small family farms remain. You no longer see the beret-wearing, sun-tanned farmers, once so typical of France. Those farming nowadays are as likely to be found working on their computers, calculating their quotas and subsidies, as cultivating the soil. Younger people are leaving farming in their droves. Thousands of farms go out of business each year.

But what chance have facts when set against the sentimental images of *la France profonde?* Holidays would be a whole lot less enjoyable without this illusion. Politicians think it does their cause no harm to keep it alive. Chirac once called farmers "the gardeners of our country and the guardians of our memory." And no politician can afford to miss the annual Paris Agricultural Show when they slap the prize-winning animals on the back and caress pretty piglets, squealing species who would much rather be let go than play this important role in the democratic process.

But getting back to Rabelais and his fun, however much he amuses the French, in the English-speaking world, he's not seen as funny at all. He's even thought to be coarse. It's a cultural thing. French humour is different from the Anglo-Saxon kind. The French love slapstick comedy, caricature and political satire. Satire thrived in revolutionary France. Satirists got great mileage from mocking the old regime. In 1832 a caricaturist, Honoré Daumer, was locked up for six months for representing King Louis Philippe as Gargantua, Rabelais' ravenous giant. Then after he abdicated, caricature enjoyed a field day and it has been prospering since. Sarkozy was a satirist's dream. And it didn't bother him. He once said he'd prefer an excess of satire to an excess of censorship.

French humour loves most of all to play with words – linguistic stunts, homonyms, onomatopoeia, spoonerisms. Because these are things that don't relocate easily into different languages, it explains why French humour doesn't travel well. There's one exception: French cartoons. Asterix has been translated into seventy languages. Along with Belgium's Tintin, it's one of the greatest successes.

Declan and Steve love Asterix and Tintin. Indeed any comic, once they get their head into it, renders them unavailable for conversation for hours. Treasa puts her lack of interest in comics down to her mother's ban on them. The visit to La Devinière got her going about her great childhood deprivation: "The other children on our road were speaking a different language from us because we weren't allowed to read comics," she said.

"And why did she not allow them?" asked Steve.

"She thought they cut out the need to read at all. All you had to do was look at the pictures."

Declan and Steve looked at one another. They seemed to be wondering what that said about them – comics' greatest fans.

"You know you can always acquire a liking for things if you really want to," suggested Declan.

But no. Treasa was determined. "It's too late now. It's something you have to be introduced to in childhood."

And so we left Chinon and La Devinière with Treasa lamenting the comic gaps of her childhood and Steve unsettled about how joyless his Calvinist forebears must have been. We were heading next to Amboise, the hub of French Renaissance vanity, a region where joy was no obstacle at all to salvation. Wine, women, royal masques, mummeries, great beauties, young courtiers, hunting and other heady delights are what are associated with Amboise. It's in the heart of the Loire Valley, the seat of power of the Renaissance prince himself, King Francis I, Rabelais' patron and great fan.

# CHAPTER 15

A perfectly crystalline summer morning and the road was ours. The classic side of the Loire was passing by, the road that links the great towns of Angers, Saumur, Blois, Chinon. This is châteaux country where royal hangers-on set up their grand dwellings when French monarchs made their home here on the banks of the Loire. Every now and then these architectural beauties peeped from between thick forest and the water's edge. They looked towards the riverside. Some were constructed before the roads and were designed to be approached from the water.

The road curved obligingly around the shapely river. If the Loire had been straight, rather than in the outline of an elbow, and not so temperamental in its flow – fast and fierce in spring and autumn, more easy-going in summer and winter – it would have been ideal for commercial use. They did try to make it navigable. As early as the fifteenth century, merchants along the route talked the King into trying to raise its banks. It failed. What a blessing. It was as if the last of France's wild rivers, as the Loire is sometimes called, plotted with nature, even elbowing kings out of its path, in insisting that its waters would be for pleasure only. And Pleasure took up the cause, in style.

There is something for everyone here. The river mellows the climate in its path, prolonging the warm influence of the Atlantic upstream. The shimmering sky above it anoints it with a special quality of light that artists love. The dense forests provide exciting hunting ground.

Without its history the Loire would be delightful. With it, the region oozes with enchantment. Here is where France's cultural journey all began: from tribal, to bloody confrontation with Roman legionaries, to Viking raids, to the spoils of war on the battlefield of Italy. It was the booty of France's Italian ventures that sowed the seeds that flowered into the French Renaissance. And you see before you, in broad daylight, the loot that was unpacked here when three kings in a row blasted their way into Italy.

Steve had calculated their youthfulness when they invaded: Charles VIII aged twenty-four; Louis XII, fairly advanced, in his mid thirties and the twenty-one-year-old Francis I. "Why then" he wondered "do we have the illusion that our age is way ahead when it comes to young decision-makers?"

Why indeed? I can't answer but perhaps youth would have been well advised to wait before making some decisions. It was said of Charles VIII, the first to set off for Italy on his "holy war", that he was the most foolish man in France, not technically an idiot but three-quarter-witted. He left Lyons on 27 July 1494 at the head of an army of forty thousand, equipped with the best artillery the world had ever known. And it excited him no end.

Italy collapsed before him. The Italian Renaissance town walls were not sturdy enough for the force of modern artillery. In the beginning it was a walkover for Charles, though in the end, France was pushed out. The blow of defeat was softened by the paintings, tapestries, manuscripts, porphyry and other gems that they managed to pillage, and this treasure and the ideas of Italy were to have a long future in their new home. The King first put them to use to beautify his castle at Amboise. It helped him to recover from the death of his only male child, something the Queen, Anne of Brittany, never got over.

Charles didn't enjoy his plunder for long. Four years later, in the spring, he was escorting his wife up a ladder by a low door into a sort of barn to watch a game of tennis from a gallery, when he struck his head against a lintel. The effect took its time in delivering its blow. He sat for a few minutes chatting, then fell into a coma. That night he was dead. He left France in debt and disorder from his Italian ventures, and without an heir. So the crown passed to his cousin, who became Louis XII.

The new King's biggest problem was the dead King's widow. Anne was fiercely patriotic about her native Brittany. Brittany was an independent duchy, a druidic land of mists and dreams. To let it loose at that point from the French Crown would have been a blow to pride and power. Brittany was to France what Ireland was to England, a Celtic people with inconvenient notions of their own identity. There was also the risk that Brittany would strike up a friendship with France's other foe, Burgundy. Burgundy had sided with the English in the Hundred Years War.

King Louis considered his problem. There was only one way out. He would have to marry Anne of Brittany. That was no great hardship; he was genuinely attracted to her. But there was one small obstacle. He was already married. His wife was Jeanne de France. Jeanne was born deformed. Her father, King Louis XI, had kept her out of sight. Her husband now told her he would rather die heirless than to displease her, which was mighty romantic of him in those demanding days of royal continuity. At the same time he promised to marry Anne of Brittany within the year or give up the four fortresses that France held in the duchy of Brittany.

A divorce was hard to get through the paces of Rome, as England's Henry VIII was to find out a few decades later. But fortune was on Louis's side. Just the right Vicar of Christ was enthroned in the Vatican – Pope Alexander VI, of the notorious Borgia family – and he knew a thing or two about the ways of the world. He was ready to do a deal. The French King could help his family's (and Pope though he was, he did have children) ambitions in Italy.

To make his case for an annulment, Louis claimed his marriage to Jeanne de France had not been consummated. That sure came as news to her. She let off some steam by breaking her lute. As tantrums go it was a mild enough one. Eventually she gave up men and worldly stuff altogether and retired to Bourges to found a convent and, happily, life worked out better for her there. She was later canonised Saint Jeanne de France.

Cesare Borgia, Pope Alexander VI's son, was only in his twenties when he arrived, in a show of great pomp, to drop off the divorce permit to Louis. Here was a young decision-maker if ever there was one. At sixteen he had been made Archbishop of Valencia and Cardinal the following year. Brash would be a muted way to describe him. His favourite tactic was to strike when the enemy was unarmed. He was thought to have murdered his own brother and his great success was the massacre at Senigallia in December 1502, when he invited his enemies to celebrate the success of their joint venture, then, during the feast, had them strangled. This was the French King's new pal. The deal between Louis and the Borgias has been described as the most cynical deal in history and really it must have been fairly high on the list of that most hotly contested of titles.

Francis I was the third king to invade Italy. His mother, Louise, urged him to be cautious, but caution didn't fit well into his young head. She made a pilgrimage on foot to Our Lady of the Fountain, which is somewhere outside Amboise, pleading for the success of her son's venture. And her prayers were answered, in the early stages of the campaign at least.

Treasa had the idea that we make enquiries about visiting this shrine, but anyone she asked gave a suitable shrug to show they had no idea. Steve and Declan showed all the signs of relief that no one was able to locate it. Steve asked Treasa if she was planning anything reckless that needed Our Lady of the Fountain's help.

The French army in the beginning had a great run of successes in Italy. Francis's arrival home to Amboise in August 1516 marked the opening moment of the Renaissance prince. On his way he made a triumphal voyage up the Rhône, stopping at Saint Baume in Provence to give thanks before the body of Mary Magdalene. (And we thought we had visited her in Vézelay.)

Francis had a lot to give thanks for – the great plunder of Italian art that he managed to get hold of – works by Raphael, Titian, da Vinci's *Mona Lisa*. His big regret was that he hadn't hauled *The Last Supper* from Milan. This loot, along with that of his predecessors, laid the basis for France's cultural blossoming. But the greatest trophy of all from Francis's Italian campaign was the great man himself, Leonardo da Vinci, brought in person from Italy, to spend the remainder of his life – which as it turned out was just three years – here in Amboise, in the service of the King of France.

I would have thought da Vinci of much more interest than Francis but it seemed that wasn't how other tourists felt, if the much longer queue for the Château of Chambord, Francis I's residence, was anything to judge by. It is the château of châteaux, outdoing all the architectural excesses of this region. We got in to Clos Lucé pretty quickly. This is the manor house beside Chambord where da Vinci lived. Da Vinci seemed an affable sort of guy. At his funeral sixty beggars followed his coffin. That was his wish. I'm not sure what their exact purpose was, but it seemed like a nice wish to have. I couldn't imagine Francis having such a humble aspiration. Clos Lucé had a cosy feel to it. Its red brick gave it a very modern look. You would believe it if you heard it had been built in the last hundred years. Its size is more manageable than Chambord too. Downstairs some models of da Vinci's designs have been constructed to prove how well they worked.

What has puzzled, indeed depressed, many generations is how multi-skilled da Vinci was. Sculptor, painter, scientist, inventor, mathematician, botanist, musician – how long a list of talents can any one man have? When you count your own little catalogue of skills alongside his, it's enough to put you in bad form. But holidays are not the time for sulking over your limitations.

Treasa wondered what made him such a freak of giftedness? "He was a vegetarian," she said, looking mischievously at Declan.

A lot of other reasons have been offered to explain his great intellect. He was the son of a notary and a peasant woman, and some put his genius down to this mix. Another possibility is that a kite fell out of the sky and hovered over his cradle when he was a baby. He himself thought it was an omen and who would argue with him?

We thought we would be able to see some of the works of art that were brought here to Amboise from Italy but when we enquired in the tourist office no one knew what we were talking about. It seems most of them went to the museums in Paris.

Apart from the cultural theft, the harvest of the French triumph in Italy did not endure. The trouble began after the election of the nineteen-year-old Charles V as Holy Roman Emperor. Without a hint of Francis's showiness, Charles ousted the French from northern Italy and they had to hightail it out of Milan. In Pavia they suffered their final defeat in 1525. And Francis, in splendid dress, was taken prisoner, humbled in front of all of Europe. I expect the finery of which he was so fond, looked not so splendid in defeat, like Cinderella hobbling home in one glass slipper. Charles characteristically didn't rejoice at having the French King as his prisoner, though there was plenty to be joyous about. Instead he prayed.

Francis played the sackcloth-and-ashes trick from his cell in Madrid. He wore cheap clothes, which must have rested uneasily on his royal body. He fasted three times a week, eating only fish. Apart from the hardship, for this great hunter, of doing without meat, fish disagreed with his stomach. *Parlement* noted the big saving in money from having this extravagant young King locked up. Then a deal was struck, an exchange for his two sons. And young François and Henri were taken into captivity for four years, something the seven-year-old Henri never got over.

The period following defeat at Pavia was a shocking time in French history. Towns were ravaged, soldiers unpaid, food taxed. The church took advantage of the chaos and arrested heretics and suppressed learning. This was Reformation France, a low moment in French history. However, other aspects of France's past soar proudly: the Enlightenment, the intellectual and cultural high-flying, the French model of civilisation, the ideals of the Revolution – liberty, equality and fraternity. Equality, especially, stands out and back at the hotel that evening we were drawn into a conversation on this very subject.

Steve was in the hotel lounge having a chat with a tall, grey-haired man, who sat very straight in his chair, when Treasa, Declan and I joined him. Steve has that kind of drawing power; people strike up conversations with him on trains, in pubs, in restaurants, anywhere. Treasa says they must find the same pull in him as insects do. And for his tolerance he often gets cornered by old bores and one-way conversationalists who rant on and on, repeating themselves wearily, giving him unsought information about a hip replacement or other installations that have made life so much better for them. It's not unusual for them to pull up the leg of a trousers and show him where they'd been knifed by some saviour surgeon who got to them just in the nick of time, as if their absence from the world would have been the worst thing that ever happened. Just as well they don't try these conversations with Declan because he faints at the mere mention of blood or anything remotely gory.

As we seated ourselves, Steve nodded in our direction to acknowledge our arrival, but the man kept on talking. We could overhear him telling about his great love for this part of France. He had been coming here since he'd retired, which I reckoned was quite a while, and staying six weeks at a time.

"The Loire to me is nature's representation of the French themselves, like as if it was shaped in their image. You know the double-sided outlook they have on life here – the lofty airs on the one hand and then their special liking for equality on the other," he said. "You know French politicians fight it out with one another as to which of them has the least interest in money. At election time they do anyway, whatever about afterwards," he nudged Steve, chuckling at his own observation.

"Did you ever hear what Hollande said, that he dislikes the rich? Wouldn't that be an extreme thing for even the leader of a socialist party to say in England?" he said, as if everyone came from England, or if they didn't that they should have.

"That he dislikes the rich," he repeated, drawing himself back to look at Steve's reaction to this outrageous idea. "But in France, it's not just politicians of the left who come out with that kind of hostility towards money, but all of them. What's this Chirac said once?" He tilted his head sideways to recall the words. Then it came to him: "that liberalism was worse than communism or something like that. But," he went on, prodding Steve in the arm, "they wouldn't say those things unless it was what the people wanted to hear. Karl Marx is well thought of here in France, you know," he said, with gravity in his voice that made you feel the quicker you got out of this subversive country the better. "He doesn't send the same shivers up the spine in France. Far from it."

Treasa asked him how the Loire represented all that, which was courageous of her, given that she hadn't been included in the conversation.

He paused thoughtfully, which made you expect a reasonable explanation. "A river comes from the same poetry, the same desire that wants equality, you see?" he answered, looking at her as if she was rather stupid not to have seen the comparison. "There's an equality about the Loire, the high-flying châteaux along its banks on the one hand, and the great interest in equality that the French have and that a river represents so well."

Steve knit his eyebrows but said nothing.

At that point Declan took his leave and went for a swim. He's not a man to suffer ramblers gladly.

What else did we learn that evening from this gentleman before his wife appeared, located him with a peer over her glasses, and hauled him off to dinner? That the three main French rivers were feminine nouns and that was the way it should be; that only the Rhône, for some odd reason, was masculine, that the Loire had the best example of womanly traits, rising humbly then getting wilder and gaining grandeur as she got to know herself, that she positioned herself neatly between north and south like an equalising arbiter between the two. Yes, she was a woman all right, a cantankerous one at that, untamable, seeing herself as providing fun for the French, from kings to peasants.

Trying and all as the conversation was, there was truth in what he said about French suspicion of wealth and that runs through their culture and their literature, from Rabelais, Molière, Zola, Maupassant to Sartre. The thing is, though heady delights are much associated with the French, they are willing to pay for a generous solidarity with their fellow countrymen. While the Anglo-Saxon world is captivated by strident capitalism, the French have always liked a kindly state. It goes back at least to Louis XIV and his finance minister, Colbert, when state money funded the construction of roads and canals and got involved in industries, from salt to tapestry. France stayed faithful to their way. In the nineteenth century, while England and the United States pulsed with private enterprise, state money built French rail and developed all kinds of industries from coalmines to banks. Today their hospitals, roads and rail are second to none. Their public debt might be high but inequality in France is not as extreme as elsewhere.

French interest in equality showed itself in style when France lost its best champion of benevolence, Abbé Pierre, in 2007. He died at ninety-four after having devoted his life to the poor. Notre Dame was chosen for his funeral. For the seven years preceding 2003, Abbé Pierre had been voted the best loved living Frenchman. That year he asked to have his name removed from the list because he disliked that kind of reverence. Then Zidane took his place as France's most beloved.

Abbé Pierre made his first mark during the awful winter of 1954, when the homeless were dying on the streets. (A film was made about it, *Hiver 54*.) His sense of anger made him storm into the studio and grab the microphone from a startled presenter at Radio Luxembourg in Paris to shout at listeners to wake up. A woman had frozen to death on the street in the small hours of that morning holding an eviction notice in her hand. His appeal stirred French scruples and the donations poured in, such that it upset the postal and phone services. Blankets, clothes, jewellery piled higher and higher in the disused railway station of Gare d'Orsay.

Though a priest, Abbé Pierre didn't mention God and that suited secular France just fine. Neither does the French benevolent state mention his name. Indeed it takes great care not to, in contrast to the American not-so-benevolent state, where the name God is never out of the vocabulary. The United States has faith in inequality. It sharpens the competitive edge, they believe. But secular France, guided by reason, not God, is not so at ease with that sort of rugged individualism.

Steve is self employed, not typically someone who should admire state interference. And he does admit that it has downsides, things like shops being told when to hold sales, a ban on below-cost selling, a limit on the number of pharmacies or taxis or whatever any one person can own. "But the French are happy with it and willing to pay for it, so why should outsiders get so worked up about it?" he said.

However, if you think that on holidays you can muscle into the French benevolent state and travel uninsured, you're wrong. You pay – and dearly at that – for any care you might need. X-rays, hospitalisation and other treatments are not for non-contributors.

The following morning we were ready to leave the Loire and head back once again towards Angers, where we would turn northwards towards Laval to visit the next place on our itinerary: Saulges.

# CHAPTER 16

I'm sure Saulges features in some guidebooks but it got no mention in ours. It's a little gem of a place in the Department of Mayenne in the northwest of France, almost straight north of Angers. It is so well endowed with sites of all ages that I can't understand how it got left out.

In the hotel we got a warm welcome from the resident dog, a little Jack Russell, who floated around the reception area. He got onto your lap with the mildest of encouragement, and sometimes without any encouragement at all. Fortunately, the weather was dry so his paws were clean. After dinner we were having a drink in the lounge and there was a moment of tension when he leapt on to Treasa's perfectly white skirt. But Steve was swift in coming to the rescue. No great hardship for him; he loves dogs and he isn't one bit fussy about his clothes.

During the day the dog could be seen sniffing around the charming old-world village, wandering around the tourist office, exploring the Gothic or Romanesque churches (I don't know which architecture smells best), balancing on his hind paws ready to return the hospitality of anyone who glanced his way.

After dinner we went for a short walk around the village. It was quiet that evening. The houses were all shuttered up. Not a single chink of light could you see escaping from a window once the shutters bolted up for the night. Just the odd car could be heard. Saulges had only one shop, a few hotels, a tourist office and two medieval churches, one Gothic, the other a small Romanesque Carolingian church. There was no bakery. Fancy that, a French village without the whiff of baking. Where do they buy their fresh bread, so indispensable to French well-being?

A strange calmness hung in the evening air, like a world that had fallen asleep, yet Saulges pulsed to its own rustic beat. Cows grazed quietly on the slanted pastures, brown and white with some Friesians mixed in. We could hear sheep bleating but none were visible.

Signposts vied with one another for attention, pointing the way by narrow byways to prehistoric, to historic, to modern, to ancient, to an early Christian oratory across a pastoral bridge, to medieval churches, to a windmill unique of its kind, to limekilns dating from tender years, and of course to the caves whose timeless origin leaves every other claim to antiquity in the shade.

The foliage gave thick coverage; only the well-hoed gardens revealed that the earth was as black here as everywhere else. Every now and then a teasing break appeared through the lush vegetation where you caught a narrow glimpse of river or sloping levels, down to some place or other that you must look into before you leave. The whispering of flowing water was rarely out of earshot.

Through the break of vegetation the ground rose and you could see distant fields, enclosures large and small, and they looked like a gallery of paintings of corn gold, of sunflower yellow, of fields faded with grass-ends exposed having been robbed of their meadows. Hay bales lay in rounds, curled like Swiss rolls in a *pâtisserie*, folded tight for winter feeding. Some trees stood huddled in thickets; others formed a single line of boundary. Here and there was an odd lone tree standing aloof from its companions, bent and undefended, like an outcast in a close-knit community. Then at the horizon's edge – hazy with distance – was a landscape in blue-grey.

Next morning the village was covered in a light mist as we headed for the caves that had brought us to Saulges in the first place. The only person in sight was a man watering hydrangeas. He could have spared himself the trouble that morning because they were already well moistened and their pink petals glistened with morning vapour. Just three of us went, Declan, Steve and I. Treasa was nursing a twisted ankle that she had injured the evening before where the ground changed levels without warning.

The visit did not run as smoothly as expected. We went to the *acceuil,* which in English would be called a reception desk. *Acceuil* is the French word for welcome. When the receptionist whom we met is on duty, they should call it the unwelcome. She was a dark-haired, pretty woman, decidedly intent on hassle, despite our lack of inclination, and frankly our lack of ability to fight in a foreign language. The hotel had booked our tour for ten o'clock. The young woman wanted proof.

"Did you not get a piece of paper from the hotel?" she barked, her dark eyes staring accusingly at me.

"No, the hotel didn't give me anything like that, I'm absolutely sure."

But she needed this piece of paper, she snarled.

I swear I was not hiding anything. I would have preferred to lie before France's investigating magistrate than to this woman.

My missing papers sounded of such a serious nature that I got the impression that without them the tour could not go ahead. There were two men sitting at a table near the reception desk and they looked passive enough, not too upset about my grave misdemeanour. Apart from the receptionist and us, they were the only people there. Then, about ten minutes and many mutterings and mumblings later, as if some great concession had been made, she agreed that we could do the tour.

If it was that easy to solve – to bypass this crucial piece of paper – the whole storm was surely unnecessary. But I didn't bring that up just in case the mighty rules of officialdom might descend upon me again and bar us from the tour. She warned that the caves were not for those who had a problem with *vertige*, that there were so many hundred steps down into the earth to be negotiated. At that point Declan opted out. He doesn't like enclosed spaces.

She drew a diagram on a piece of paper and began an onslaught of instructions on how we were to get there, in her fastest native French, little of which I caught. But no matter how little I grasped

I wasn't going to risk asking her to repeat them. I had interrupted her day seriously enough without provoking her further. I did, however, chance to ask why she was in such bad form. After all, we only came to do a tour, not to ransack the place. And she said, "Because you don't understand what I'm saying."

Ah, OK. That, right enough, was a good reason to be in bad form and it helped me enormously to understand French with greater clarity. Then she told us, with a gust of urgency, that the tour began at ten and that we had to get over to the far side of the field. That would have been some achievement because it was, by then, several minutes past ten.

We tore across the damp grass expecting to see at least a dozen people waiting at the cave's mouth, ready to devour us for having held them up. Or worse still, they might have already begun the tour and we would have had to make our way into the bowels of the earth on our own. So when we arrived, in a serious state of breathlessness, you can imagine our surprise to find the gate to the cave locked and no one there. Surely we must be in the wrong place, we thought, but Declan, who had come along with us to the entrance, guaranteed that this was indeed the only gate to the cave. Several minutes later the guide strolled along at his ease and opened the cave. It was then we realised he was one of the two men who had been sitting at the table in the *acceuil* while the receptionist fought it out with us. And we learned also that we were the only people taking the tour.

Walking gingerly through narrow passages about fifteen metres deep, guarding our heads from knife-edge stones, we got a tour of Grotte de Rochefort. We could feast our eyes on this underground sculpture to our hearts' content. These caves were known to prehistoric man and when you see this underground of carvings it would somehow wipe the smug smile of modern speed off your face. Our age loves haste, having all the information ever known to man at the click of a mouse, instant conversation to the furthest point on the earth. But life down here has no time for that sort of pace at all.

125

For an unimaginable number of years the unseen sculptors of dripping water and chalky rock together made fanciful shapes. Stalactites and stalagmites gave and received repeatedly and spectacularly until no artist could have bettered the lacework of rock they created. Such a remarkable formation of caves and canyons is unusual for this part of the country. About twenty caves have been found at the foot of the cliffs here bordering the valley of the River Erve (though only two can be visited: Rochefort and Margot). They cover a distance of a kilometre and a half or so.

In the later morning, when we did the tour of Margot's cave, the crowds had gathered, so this time we didn't have the benefit of individual attention. This cave was called after a local young woman who, back in late medieval times, walked from village to village begging. At night she took refuge in the cave. Caves were then thought to lead straight to hell, so locals suspected her of being a witch, as only they could in those distrusting days, when anyone behaving oddly was chosen for the stake. She always carried a black hen. The villagers kept a watchful eye on her. One night they saw her entering the cave and seconds later they heard a terrifying noise, felt shaking of the earth and saw black smoke coming from the entrance. That, naturally enough, gave them something to talk about. An arrangement had been reached with the devil, they had no doubt. The pact was, Margot told them later, that if she agreed to leave the cave for seven days, on her return she would find treasure. She went back on the seventh day. Gathered villagers waited for her to emerge. But she never did.

When it is damp in La Grotte Margot you can see a twinkling of light on the ceiling which looks a bit like gold. But it's nothing more than droplets of water that form on the rock. Maybe the young woman mistook them for treasure. Whether Margot's was one of the bodies, dating from the Middle Ages, recovered in 1924 – one female and two male – or whether there was any truth in the story at all, we don't know. But one way or another, the cave still bears her name.

Up until the nineteenth century, people sacrificed black chickens and other black animals in Margot's cave. The belief was that this ritual would make you rich.

Before leaving I went back to the *accueil* to ask the rude receptionist her name. I had every intention of complaining about her. As I walked through the doorway she asked me breezily if I'd had a good tour. Finding out her name seemed all of a sudden out of place. And she gave it to me without the least hesitation. The thing is the French take these little outbursts in their stride, like a game, a moment of bad humour. So what? Shrug shrug. If this happened in the Anglo Saxon world you would have a barrage of complaints, training programmes on customer relations put in place, letters of explanations for wounded feelings. But the French are easy-going about it. They don't take those rants too seriously. Maybe they're right.

After lunch we set off on a delightful trail recommended by the sunny woman in the tourist office. It loops its way around the village by the river. The harsh heat of afternoon sun is not our favourite time for walking, but the little lanes were so lusciously shaded by foliage that tilted towards the centre to form a leafy parasol, that we thought we could ignore the hour of the day.

Our path took us by the tiny oratory dedicated to Saint Cénéré at the top of a few steps, along by box hedging and beneath a tree. Here among the green and mossy growth, beside the water, this saint came around 650 AD to live a hermetic life. We had to wait our turn to go in to the oratory because it holds only a handful of people. There was a representation of the saint – well I presume it was he, a white bearded man in cloaks with a hermetic appearance and looking very like a saint to me – behind the altar in very modern colours of pink and green.

You could not have chosen a better spot for a contemplative life. Even today the air breathes pure in Saulges and it has a hush of peace about it that brings to mind otherworldly longings. The old feels embalmed here, sealed, as if past and present are rolled into one. We passed by an old mill, a stone house with a roof shaped like a bonneted woman. A mix of wild and cultivated flowers in pink and red lined the way. We breathed the fleeting damp fragrance of the withered scrub, because here the sun's rays cannot always reach through the thick undergrowth. Some of the deeper vegetation may not have been touched by sunlight since the time of Saint Cénéré. The flora around Saulges is uncommon for western France and the limestone formation is unusual for these parts too. I'm convinced hermetic people sought out places where the earth did free-thinking things, refused to follow normal patterns, like they themselves opted out of the beaten track. No doubt it brought its own harvest in exchange for what they gave up.

All was going wonderfully well until our umbrella of foliage came to an end. The map showing the circle of walkway hadn't warned us. It gave no indication of the length of the walk either. There were unexpected turns, which upset even Declan's bearings, and it was a whole lot longer than it looked, which was a worry for Treasa and her aching ankle. I thought for a while we would have to carry her back to the hotel. It seemed ridiculous to be going astray in such a small place. I spotted a man on a tractor and I went to ask him the way, but by the time I got there he had driven to the far side of the field. We sighed with relief when we saw a large group of people walking towards us and we hoped they knew where they were going. They directed us to the hotel and we were happy to see the spire and roofs of the little village of Saulges again. We went back to the hotel where Treasa rested her ankle.

Later that evening, when we arrived for dinner in a hotel recommended by the woman in the tourist office, a few kilometres from Saulges, everything was locked up. We roamed around, trying this door and that, looking through glass panels to see if there was any sign of life but there was no one in sight – no guests, no staff, no human life at all. For a while we wondered if we had got our times wrong. All was well in the end though. The door was unlocked. Dinner was delicious.

Our only difficulty that evening was that we had to do battle with the waitress who was intent on speaking English. It's funny, if you were to break into English in France, not a single word would you get out of them, even if they were fluent English speakers. That's fair enough. I think it's the height of bad manners to burst into your own language in a foreign country, without asking anyone if they understand you. But they don't always allow you the same consideration in return. They often take one look at your pale and freckled face, at skin that looks as if it has not seen the light of sun save for the few weeks you've spent in France, and they ignore your arduous efforts at their language and answer you blithely in English. It's quite easy to give up the struggle, especially if their English is better than your French. Not Treasa. She goes into convoluted explanations that, since she is now in a French-speaking country, that French has a sort of right of way. That evening she didn't bother with her usual explanation because it never works anyway. She just said: "We're not English."

The waitress apologised for her assumption and addressed us from then on in French. As we were leaving, she asked, "What nationality are you?"

"We're Irish," we explained.

"But I thought English was the language spoken in Ireland?"

"So it is but we don't, not while we're on holidays," answered Treasa. When she was outside she said: "What I said was technically correct, wasn't it?"

"I think it stretched the technical a few yards," said Declan. "Or metres even."

Next morning we made our way to nearby Jublains. Not to include Saulges in a guidebook is an oversight; not to have Jublains is ridiculous because the traces of the Roman presence in Gaul are so well preserved here. There was no scarcity of granite around these parts and, after their conquest, the Romans used it for a big urbanisation project. It looks in a wonderful state of repair, considering that it dates to the first century AD – the temple, the theatre, the forum and the thermal baths, all connected by paved roads. The amphitheatre overlooks the basin of the Evron River and is on a natural slope, which gave spectators a good view. That morning the chain of hills in the distance were coloured in an inky blue, far enough away to look sheltering yet not so near as to be imposing.

When evangelising Christians arrived, they disliked thermal baths and statues of false gods so they wiped them out with their own layer of civilisation. They built a church on top of the thermal centre. Now only the underground part of the Roman baths is visible. We viewed it through a glass panel from the basement of the church. There was nobody around when we visited, so we let ourselves in and pressed a button that gave us a full account of the history. It was handy because we couldn't wait for the official opening hours.

Our next stop was Alençon, to visit the lace-making museum there. It is a hobby of Treasa's. She goes to lace-making classes, though she says, in all her years learning, she has never produced anything of any practical use. But she likes the achievement of doing such intricate work. It was late afternoon when we arrived, and by the time we found where the *Musée de la Dentelle* (lace museum) was it was nearly closing time. We had a mere twenty minutes to do a tour. Still, they charged us the full price, €4.00, not a lot, admittedly, but there was the small matter of principle. The tour included a film show which we couldn't possibly have seen in twenty minutes and do the tour as well. We didn't want to waste too much time arguing because the minutes were passing. So we paid, protesting in our limited French about their unfairness. But the people at the reception desk were unimpressed with our argument. The men hadn't come along, which was a relief. They wouldn't have enjoyed it and it would have doubled the injustice of having to pay full price.

Alençon was an important centre of lace-making going back to the seventeenth century, when Jean-Baptiste Colbert established a Royal workshop here in the town to produce Venetian-style lace, so that the French court of Louis XIV wouldn't have to import it. Soon they developed their own particular method of lace-making, and this style came to be called the "queen of lace".

The exhibits inside glass casing were fine and intricate. One rounded lace display was called a *volant*. I knew *volant* was the word for the steering wheel of a car but I couldn't make out how you could apply it to lace. When I asked the two people who were working there, they shrugged to tell me they didn't know. A client overheard my question and she explained that it was a border of lace for the edge of a skirt. My idea of a steering wheel seemed funny. "It's for steering your petticoat in the right direction," whispered Treasa, and we both giggled.

On our way back to the hotel we visited the town's church. The French saint, Thérèse of Lisieux, was baptised here and her lace christening robe was on display on the wall. It was ornate, which was hardly surprising because her father was in the lace business in this town. He later moved the family to Lisieux and began a workshop there.

Every pew in the church was full. There was a service going on and a lot of eager singing. Someone handed us leaflets with the names Zélie and Louis Martin in bold print. These were the parents of Saint Thérèse and the service was a celebration of their lives. So many clergy were participating that those on the outer edges of the altar steps looked as if they might heave over the line. Not so for the main celebrant, a cardinal, recognisable by his red hat, who occupied the central position. We didn't stay long. All we wanted was to have a quick look around. Our departure – all four of us – looked out of line with the general zeal of the crowd.

Next morning I woke early, so I sneaked out of bed without wakening the whole hotel, or crashing into anything as usually happens when I'm trying to be quiet. With the extra slice of day I'd gained, I went to the early morning chanting in the Carmelite convent. These nuns once played a big role in the town. When, after the Revolution, the demand for lace dropped, the special technique of Alençon lace-makers was nearly lost, but the sisters saved it.

To be up in a town still asleep was blissful, a moment when the sounds and motions of morning performed their show for me alone. Pieces of litter and tinfoil wrappings from the night before blew in the breeze, making faint rasping noises along the empty pavement. Some got cornered in shop alcoves or caught behind electricity poles only to break free again and go on their rambling way. Traffic lights went red and green, they rang out their pedestrian chimes although they signalled no one to stop or go. Everything seemed unperturbed by its purposeless action. The odd sound of a car engine hummed in the distance. Birds filled the air with their song. Later they would have to compete with the mechanised noise of the working day but now the world was theirs to serenade at their ease.

Solitude had one downside that morning. There was not a person in sight to ask for directions to the convent. In my tiptoeing effort to get out without causing disturbance, I hadn't taken the details of where it was located. Finally, I caught a glimpse of a man walking a frisky-looking puppy, about to turn around a corner. I ran to catch up with him. He couldn't place where the convent was for a minute or two but then he remembered and he called after me and showed me the way. It was just around the corner from where we stood.

As I turned the handle softly, the voice of the Carmelite beginning-of-day floated through the crack of open door, female chants in unison. Like the birds make their daily claim to their patch of world with their song, the nuns make their daily renunciation of the world with theirs. There were four of them, all old, dressed in beige cotton veils and long robes. One played an organ. They stood, knelt and sat, stood again and knelt in orderly sequence. All this ritual – standing, kneeling, sitting, bowing, standing again – probably had more meaning in the days when they were a large congregation. Now just four were left to chant alone and the gestures looked diluted.

On my way back, as I approached the hotel, deep in thought about the difficulty of staying loyal to religious vows put to the test of a long lifetime, I heard Treasa calling me. She was putting her bag in the boot. "Where did you get to?"

When I told her, she said: "That's such a pity. If I'd known I'd have gone too."

I felt as if I'd done something sly, going off to the convent to hear the chants on my own, not inviting anyone to share my secret joy. I liked my moment of solitude, of doing something just for myself, an early hour unshared with the rest of humanity. There's nothing more balancing than to opt out of the crowd for a brief moment; that is, provided you can rejoin them when you've had enough of your own company. An entire life on your own, now that is a test of a different order. I guess that's what distinguishes us fair-weather soloists from the hermetic types.

Declan and Steve were at the door waiting to leave. Soon we were on the road, driving northwest, towards our next destination: Coutances Cathedral

# CHAPTER 17

Our drive took us by Domfront approaching Normandy, back once again in the land of steep inclines and broad horizons. On the slopes of the hills farmland was showing off its fertility in contrast to the burned grass further south. Acres of fields were in tillage. Further in the distance dairy cows dotted the fields. Skies looked wilder than in the south as the strokes of white cloud flowed briskly in the breeze. On high ground wind turbines were moving energetically. The difference in geology between north and south was showing off in the roof-tops. This far north they use slate from the plentiful supplies of the quarries of the north. The grey roofs look less warm than the red-roofed tradition of the south. Red clay holds the warm colour of the southern sun in which they were baked.

South and north differ in personality too. Southerners think the north is cold and dreary compared to their side of the country. The south is the land of the vine, of sun, of fun, the land of the *langue d'oc*, the language of troubadour poetry. The north is the land of wheat, sugar beet, milk, the home of standard French, the *langue d'oil*. Wheat and milk give us our daily bread but wine and sun fuel the vigour. Steve says it's like the difference between the daily devotion of the spouse and the gush of the lover, though he insists he's not speaking from personal experience.

Some think it was Zola's novels, works like *Germinal,* that linked the north forevermore with gloom. It was written in the late nineteenth century and set around the coalmines of Valenciennes and it hadn't one cheerful word to say. (The woman we met in the hotel in Abbeville must have been in a serious state of moroseness after reading three of Zola's novels.) But associations put there by fiction can equally be shifted by fiction. The film *Bienvenue chez les ch'tis* (*Welcome to the Sticks*) was released in 2008 and it had a big influence in defrosting the frozen-tundra image southerners had about the north. It's about a post office manager who tries to con his way into getting a transfer to the south and, for his deceit, he's banished to cold and miserable Lille. But he soon finds out that the dismal picture he had of the place was far from true, that it's a place of fun and friendliness. Lille got a big boost as a tourist destination as a result. Tourism to Lille now compares well with that of the Loire valley. There are a few reasons other than the film, but it did make its contribution as an ambassador for the place.

Mont Saint-Michel came into view, saluting us from its height. It was looking magical with the sea in the background catching the light like cut crystal. Avranches was next, a town built on high ground. This is Plantagenet country once again, where Henry II went through a public scourging for his sin against Becket, which absolved him and brought him back to the fold of Rome. I was afraid to comment on this piece of history in case it would flare up Steve's allergy to the Plantagenets. Coutances is a straight road north of Avranches and soon the Norman spires of the cathedral were in view. Coutances is one of the procession of cathedral spires from Bayeux to Mont Saint-Michel and Chartres.

Grace and elegance come to mind with all Gothic, but in Coutances the words strike with more force. The interior reminds me of a woman in flowing robes. It makes Steve think of tall ships. He need say no more. To compare it to a ship – his great love – is enough to show how he rates it.

Windows are tall and narrow and the place exudes more height and stateliness than the others, more so than the Gothic of Notre Dame in Paris or Chartres. Yet Coutances Cathedral is said to be the least-well-known masterpiece of Gothic architecture. From certain angles it looks exaggerated, cartoon-like and mystical.

Gothic made stone pretend it was fragile, transformed it into a state of make-believe, only that the magic wand of the real medieval world was a lot more laborious. When you think about it, you can nearly hear the hammers and chisels hacking, hewing, honing, carving the great boulders into shapes that made them look malleable as baker's dough.

The centre of the cathedral brightens beneath the beams of light gathered up by the lantern tower, from its fifty-seven-metre height, and drops onto the part of the choir where the clergy used to sing hymns of praise while Mass was being celebrated on the high altar. And you fancy you can hear the male-voiced choristers, their song gathering power in its unity, in their starched vestments – deacons, archdeacons, seminarians in cassocks, rochets, surplices, woven in the best lacework northern France could offer.

Having the lantern tower as the main feature was a Norman church-building detail. In fact, all the decoration here is said to be very Norman. The lantern tower is octagonal with a circle in the centre, carefully created to show man his place in the world. The circle symbolises heaven – eternity, without end. The earth is represented by a square – with all the awkward corners life in this world can put you into. The octagonal shape stands for the resurrection. This mystical symbolism must have made heaven and its opposite number, damnation, a looming presence in daily life.

Such threats did not bother the French revolutionaries, though, and they used this lovely building as a grain store, which was a bit wicked of them, no matter how hostile they were to religion. They also scolded the statues severely to make them more amenable to the new secularism. They took them from their niches and slashed them with swords for having led people astray for so long. That would surely teach them a lesson. Later the building was used as a theatre and finally a Temple of Reason. Reason didn't suit it either, because the sentiment of Gothic belongs more to the heart than to the head.

Despite all this roughing up, the windows held out, even escaping the Allied bombings of World War II. Bombs were placed strategically so that no harm would come to architectural beauties and the stained glass of Coutances remains intact.

I bought a book from a student, who had set up a stand in the nave of the cathedral. I was taken aback when he said he was English. It was depressing to compare my poor standard of fluency to his, but I took heart when he told me his mother was French. The choice of publications was limited to a few slim outlines of the cathedral's history.

One of the things I read that made me smile was that Coutances Cathedral looks as good today as it did eight hundred years ago. How does anyone know, since no one has lived that long? But it did bring to mind how many multiples of years the skill of man outlasts man himself.

We had planned to be in Bayeux by evening, and so we saw little more of the town of Coutances. We were ready to move off once again to face the great swathes of French landscape. In this side of the country, Basse Normandie, so many places, inscriptions and memorials bear American names – Patton, Eisenhower, Kennedy – that it looks as if the United States single-handedly liberated France in 1944. (I feel sure de Gaulle would have a thing or two to say about that one. And as for the part Poland played, well nobody – but nobody – feels like recalling that.)

Declan wondered what the Americans did to make the French so grateful? "What did President Kennedy do for them?" he asked as he read a street named in his honour.

It would make you wonder if the French are quite so allergic to the United States as they sometimes profess to be. They throw a tantrum from time to time about American-style capitalism, American-style junk food. McDonald's is a common target, though it reports lively profits from its French markets. Hollywood blockbusters upset them too, though they do well at the French box office. And two avenues dedicated to American presidents – Avenue Franklin D. Roosevelt and Avenue du Président Wilson – run through the centre of Paris.

Soon we were within sight of Bayeux where we planned to spend the next few days.

# CHAPTER 18

Bayeux takes only seconds to charm you. It's the most delightful of northern towns. No matter when you visit, leisurely crowds hang around the long street that forms the centre. They lounge on the green spaces and dawdle around little lanes or on the rustic-looking bridge and this gives the place an air of permanent leisure. Along the main street, straight as a ruler and tilting into a gentle rise at one end, restaurants, cafés, bistros and craft shops line the way. Fleeting glimpses of boutique window displays make your head hum with plans of buying and dining.

Bayeux is just seven miles inland. It was part of the coastal defence as far back as Roman times and as recently as World War II. It is only when you think of all the cities along by the English Channel that were pulped in the bombing of Normandy that you feel grateful that Bayeux is still standing. It was the first city of the Battle of Normandy to be liberated and it was here de Gaulle made his first major speech on 16 June 1944. Tourists no doubt come here in their droves just to soak in the easy-going ambience of the place, but Bayeux has three major draws: the cathedral, the tapestry and the war cemetery.

The cathedral does not announce itself like other churches of its rank, but reveals its presence subtly and gradually, weaving and folding into its surroundings, making it part of a community of buildings. You can catch tiny glimpses of one or other of its flying buttresses from almost anywhere in the town. From some angles it looks like the wings of a great bird clutching her young.

Cobbled lanes run off at odd angles around the town centre,

meandering leisurely, sloping into narrow paths. Like the tributaries of a river, they look unplanned. But there is a design about their designlessness and they bring alive the spirit of how the town took shape, street by street. Cathedrals gave rise to a hierarchy of ranks and grades – bishops, canons, deans, vice-deans, cantors, vice cantors – and the architecture of this ladder of command is in full view. Rue des Chanoines (Canons' Street) has fine examples of where the higher clergy lived according to the power they wielded. The homes of the lesser clergy are smaller and prettier and look more in keeping with the rambling lanes and cobbles.

The date of the consecration of the cathedral, 14 July 1077, struck up an uncanny link with future generations. Isn't it interesting that 14 July, Bastille Day, now the most celebrated holiday on the French calendar, was the day chosen? It was as if, when they built the cathedral back in the eleventh century, they foresaw the heady day when revolutionaries would storm the Bastille some seven hundred years later. The attendance at that great event in Bayeux on "Bastille Day" 1077 included Odo, Bishop of Bayeux; his half brother, William Duke of Normandy or William the Bastard, as he was known. But that day he had shed his slighting name, and bore the more splendid one of William the Conqueror, which he had earned in 1066 when he conquered England in the Battle of Hastings. William's wife, Matilda, was there too. The cathedral then was not quite as you see it now. The largest part of what is visible today dates from the thirteenth century.

I love the cathedral's entrance. I think it is because there aren't several steps to climb and this adds the warmth of accessibility. As we walked up the aisle, shafts of afternoon sunlight were shining through the high windows and the rays, having bathed the ceiling in light, rested on the pews on the far side. The stonework between the high row of windows and the arches along the nave is finely decorated in lace-like patterns.

Like in Coutances, there was surprisingly little literature on the cathedral except for a little booklet giving a brief outline of its history and architecture. It is not like Chartres, where a whole industry of written and visual information is for sale in the cathedral shop. Even a map of the general layout was hard to come by. Finally, Declan spotted one on a wall – a fire escape plan.

I interrupted a teacher who was highlighting the main features of the building to his class of about ten-year-olds, to ask him if he knew where the labyrinth was. I expected to find it in a prominent place. He didn't know and he had to admit that in front of his pupils. I hoped I hadn't punctured his pride. He pointed to a woman in a grey suit who might help. The labyrinth, she explained, was in the chapter house and it was locked. What a pity. I was becoming quite a fan of labyrinths. Minutes later Steve read in the little booklet we had bought that the labyrinth in Bayeux differed from most cathedrals in that it was not in the nave.

The grey-suited woman went to great trouble to show us where the window commemorating the D-Day landing was. I think she thought that would make up for the lack of labyrinth, but as far as I was concerned, though I did try to look eager about her efforts, such a recent addition didn't hold the same intrigue as the other examples of antiquity around me.

Cathedrals sometimes bring to mind severe thoughts, flashbacks of all the preaching you've heard against the evils of thinking too much of yourself rather than of others, cheating, telling lies, being over-showy (though cathedrals were no example of modesty themselves), worrying about what you'll eat or drink or about what you'll wear. Was not life more important than food and the body more important than clothes, you were asked in serious tones? Little of that you heeded, and if you did, I bet you would have been outright winner of the dullest-individual-in-the-school contest.

A bird flying frantically around the cathedral reminded me of the biblical advice to consider the birds in the air and take example from them. They sowed not, nor did they reap, nor did they store away in barns. Yet they got fed. I must admit I didn't then or haven't since discovered anything practical in that advice, though I was as interested as the next in shedding my worries. And in any case this bird in the cathedral seemed to be not as fretless as the bible claimed birds to be. He looked nervous about being caught in an enclosed space. Treasa wondered if she could rescue him, but when he flew up to one of the top-row windows, she realised how useless her efforts were.

"Don't worry about him," Declan quipped. "He came in deliberately; he's a bird of prey."

The following morning we went to the Musée de la Tapisserie to see the celebrated Bayeux Tapestry. If they didn't push the cathedral to its best commercial use, they certainly did not neglect advertising the tapestry. Copies are reproduced a million fold in tablecloths, serviettes, pottery, souvenirs of all kinds in the museum shop.

I love the mellow tones of the tapestry: russet, terracotta, beige, straw gold, brown, olive green, light blue. It brings to mind autumn, harvest moons, the faded abundance that the earth gushes forth at the back end of the year. The tapestry has the same fragrant hues as Bayeux itself: the brownish waters of the River Aure that passes beneath the bridge in the town centre, and the faint russet tones of the cathedral. It reminds you of the Battle of Hastings, fought in autumn – on 16 October to be precise – the feast of Saint Michael the Archangel. They would have done nothing then without enlisting the help of the saints, no matter how rough the venture.

The tapestry recounts, in a length of seventy metres or so, the events leading up to Hastings in more than fifty scenes. Steve said it was like a strip cartoon. And indeed they advertise it as an animated cartoon from the Middle Ages. I was afraid Treasa was going to launch into more regrets about her childhood ban on comics but she didn't this time.

For all its claims, the Bayeux tapestry is not a tapestry at all. It's a work of embroidery done with coloured wool on linen. Essentially it was a piece of propaganda, to celebrate and to shape opinion on the conquest of England. Legend has it that it was commissioned by Queen Matilda and it is often referred to as *La Tapisserie de la Reine Mathilde*. But more likely it was the Bishop of Bayeux, Odo, who ordered it to adorn his cathedral. Nuns in some convent in the south of England, around the Kent area, are thought to have got the commission. Anglo-Saxon needlework was known across Europe at the time for its quality.

The tapestry's most important scene, a scene that is reproduced in the cathedral, is Harold's oath. Harold was the man most expected to take the throne of England in January 1066, and here in Bayeux, William is said to have forced him to make a promise. The two men are shown meeting, and Harold swearing an oath over holy relics. Although from the tapestry you don't know what is being pledged, the oath it seems was broken and that gave William a chance to discredit Harold as a perjurer and usurper. A broken oath taken over relics gave the Pope (Alexander II) the opening he needed to take sides, and he blessed William and offered him the papal banner. William couldn't have asked for a better sponsor, and the conquest became a holy event.

You can't escape the theme of war around Bayeux between Hastings and the Normandy landing. We stayed in the Churchill Hotel, and glass casings of war memorabilia (of Normandy, not Hastings) are placed along the corridors: pictures of the D-Day landing – *le Jour J* – uniforms, boots, helmets, belts, pictures of GIs, photos of sweethearts (it's funny how the word sweetheart is mostly associated with the lonely soldier). All the images are happy ones. You nearly get the impression that no one died at all, that is until you see all the signs pointing to cemeteries around here.

Next day we made a trip to Caen. It is about thirty kilometres from Bayeux and there's a regular train service. Even in these great days of transport, there's still a magic about the train. "It's not just the whistle, it's the smell of the rail tracks, the long trailing approach, the passing… " I didn't catch the remainder of Treasa's long list of reasons why she loved rail transport because her words got drowned out by the coming train, but I agreed with all of those I'd heard. Maybe it is the idea of community, of sharing, that is its appeal.

Steve says he still misses the chug, that trains have lost a lot of their lull since they welded the tracks together. In the old days the gap between the pieces of track, to allow for expansion, gave the movement a reassuring rhythm.

There was more sharing than usual on this train. A class of English pupils was on a school tour. One of the teachers was very talkative and she made sure that all the passengers were going to enjoy the educational aspects of the day.

"Children, look at the countryside. Look at nature. It's wonderful," she said. "Look children, see the cattle in the fields. What's a baby cow called? You should know that by now, how to identify animals and their babies. We've done that in… What's a baby horse called? Look at the map dear, you're doing map skills at school. What does itinerary mean?"

Then she turned her attention to one of the drowsy pupils. "There's Amy sleeping. Are you tired Amy darling?"

I was half expecting little Amy to ask: Why else would I be sleeping?

"I wonder if Amy's dreaming?" she said. "Do you dream darling? Do you have dreams like Alice in Wonderland?" asked the teacher, focusing on someone else.

"My cat will miss me," said a little voice from behind my seat. "Daisy-Bell knew I was going. She saw me opening my case."

"Isn't she the clever cat, Sophie," replied the teacher. "Do you have a cat Justin?" He didn't, and so we were spared any description of Justin's pet's insightfulness.

"Is it time to eat our sandwiches yet?" asked another small voice.

"No, not yet darling. What country are we in children?"

"France," they all agreed.

"Can you think of a limerick with France in it? Do you know what a limerick is?" She offered a sample: "There was a boy who could dance. He came from a place called France."

Steve whispered roguishly, "That's a lousy limerick."

Treasa elbowed him into silence.

"Do you know where Limerick is?" the teacher asked. No one knew, so she told them.

"It's in Ireland."

"My daddy says he doesn't like Ireland," announced a little male voice.

143

Beneath lowered eyebrows, the four of us shared a quiet glance.

"Oh we mustn't say that dear," said the teacher. "Do try and keep your luggage under your seats children."

We got out at Caen and left the passengers heading for Paris to enjoy the rest of the school tour. It had been my idea to spend the day in Caen to see the Abbaye aux Dames (the Women's Abbey). Queen Matilda is buried there, but more interesting are the legends that surround its foundation. One says that it was to make up for the sin of marrying a family relative that William the Conqueror and Matilda were impelled to establish this abbey. There was a papal ban on their marriage because of consanguinity. But a more colourful tale is that William pulled Matilda off her horse by the hair and dragged her all the way from Caen to the site of the abbey for calling him a bastard. To make up for his stormy outburst, he founded the abbey.

We walked from the station. It was a fairly short distance but it would have been quite a long journey if you were being dragged by the hair.

After a look around the Abbaye aux Dames and Matilda's tomb, we found an exhibition in another wing of the building. Some of the paintings were done by some of the luminaries of the Impressionist movement. It was interesting that they weren't guarded securely in some grand gallery, just hanging casually in a room for anyone to wander into.

Later we made the climb up the hill in the city centre to see the château that dominates Caen. It's a reminder that not everything in this city was flattened in the Normandy bombings. It has got through many wars unscathed. It dates from the eleventh century and is one of the largest fortified enclosures in Europe. They were cleaning the church of Saint Pierre as we passed by. About half of it was finished, looking beautifully whitened, like a toothpaste ad. We stood to admire the contrast. Declan reckoned that knocking the surface off with such aggressive sandblasting is too high a price to pay for whiteness. Then the three of us, sheepishly, backtracked on our admiration.

Rue Vaugueux is in the old part of Caen, part of the original city that managed to escape the heavy bombardment. We made a random choice from the long line of restaurants. After lunch we went for a leisurely stroll to have a look around the town before we headed for the station to take the train back to Bayeux.

There was no shortage of people in SNCF (the French railway system) uniforms around the station. It was like another era, because it's so rare nowadays to see staff at all at stations, let alone in such numbers. This is one of the joys of the French large public sector. Information got from live people is more reassuring than what you get from written timetables on walls – some of them hopelessly out of date – or even from the more up-to-the-minute monitors placed at neck-creaking heights over platforms. They confirmed – all three of them – that the stationary train at the platform was ours.

Passengers were reading, playing games, listening to music, using iPads, iPods, E-readers and doing all those *E* things that have caused the screen to replace the page. Not a magazine or book was in sight. Some things have not changed though. People rested their grimy shoes on the seats opposite them. It seems to be a universal habit. It crosses generations, cultures and genders. And good people who read from real pages and follow traditional manners have to suffer. It was better to look out the window and pretend you didn't see them.

The view was lulling. Hedges combined with speed made them look like a tapestry of woven greenery. As the train pulled out into big countryside, the full flush of summer breathed a great exhalation from the railway edge all the way to the horizon. The sun was casting darkened shadows on the east side of the hills while it warmed the curves on their western flank, choosing one over the other – like an unfair parent – elongating its reach just for the favourites. Houses passed by with windows thrown open to catch the last rays of day. The summer foliage of the trees had covered up the hard work of winter. Lovely and all as the greenery was, it was a shame to hide the complex mesh of spine-work that trees reveal in winter. A row of poplars growing on a hillside made directly for the light – erect and elegant – despite the slanting ground beneath their feet. On flatter terrain another row was lined up straight as soldiers awaiting a guard of honour inspection.

Some wild flowers had taken root by the embankment, in a secret place where no one had planted them or given them a name. These orphans showed a firm resolve to exist and bloom. They grabbed a piece of earth to land their progeny, in a small spot where man had not managed to stake a claim.

Far-off villages of stone houses topped with spires lazed in the distance. How teasing it all looked as we sped by. It put wistful thoughts in my head of coming back one day to see how these far-off roads all ended. Declan looked in their direction and took out his map.

The countryside takes the brunt of some of our comforts. Pylons, electric cables and masts marched across the fields in parallel, sharp as arrows, so out of tune with the curves and intentions of nature. This is the price passing passengers pay for electronic reading and mobile chats. Of course the train itself was a wound on the landscape when it first appeared, in straight Cartesian lines across the countryside. It spoiled a lot of local lore too. Before rail blanketed the land, regions had their own time, calculated on when night fell. Trains needed a national timetable and so a national time was imposed and local sunsets got shafted in favour of the common hour. That was only the start of it. Common markets, common currencies had all yet to come. Globalisation was the tidal wave that would knock us all into unison.

The Churchill Hotel in Bayeux was not chained up in a family of global sameness. It was solidly French. They followed the old ways. It reminded you of a place your parents would have taken you. They served coffee in silver pots and you were asked to hang up your heavy key each time you left the premises. No such concession to modernity as electronic key cards. They bowed respectfully towards the spirit of Bayeux: the cathedral, the tapestry, the war memorials.

It was our last evening in Bayeux. About half a dozen others were in the hotel lounge when we went for an after-dinner drink. They were all sitting at individual tables, on computers, mobile phones, connecting up to their distant friends. Steve commented that the great gift of being able to make contact with people on the far side of the globe cuts out the need to talk to the person alongside you.

"Exactly," said Declan wryly. "That's why I refuse to use a sat nav, so I can make my contribution in keeping alive the human touch."

But he was not convincing Treasa. "As if you'd do something so humiliating as to ask for directions," she said.

We left Bayeux next morning with the easy charm of the place still clinging to us like static electricity. But a few kilometres on the motorway is one sure way of dispersing this pleasant residue, and the opposite takes hold: of speed, of getting there, of Treasa's dreaded arrivalism.

# CHAPTER 19

We took the road we had come by nearly three weeks earlier: by Calvados, a region known for its cider, its soft cheeses and its apple brandy. But we wouldn't be stopping along the way to sample these delicacies. Our next stop was Montreuil-sur-mer and we wanted to get there reasonably early. Our timing worked out precisely except for when we arrived, an antique fair was going on in the town.

It happens once a year, on 14 July, Bastille Day, when Montreuil-sur-mer hosts a *foire brocante* (antique fair). When we booked Le Coq Hôtel months earlier they had warned us about this event. They told us to tell the person at the barrier we needed to get to the hotel and they would let us through. It all sounded very straightforward. We got the impression that the antique market would consist of a few stands, we hadn't thought it would take over the town. There was no way you could have driven through. Not at least without taking a few stalls with you, or crushing some items of timeless value beneath your wheels.

We walked to the hotel, a good twenty minutes from where we had to park. You've never seen such a collection. Displays were tightly lined along the street. Items ranged from old jumble to aged valuables, arranged in stalls, some strewn on to the pavement. Some fine china was in perfect condition, others with cracks and missing handles looked the worse for wear. Ancient pictures of hunts, stags and hounds; lamps, brass-work, silverware spilt over their allotted areas. You had to be careful where you placed your foot. It was all very lovely, traditional, nostalgic. I don't know how long they have been hosting this event and we were in no humour for finding out when we arrived at the hotel, sore-footed and tired.

We protested at not having been told more clearly. We explained how much it had put us out to have to walk all the way. We complained that we had no access to our bags, apart from walking to the car and carrying them back to the hotel. The proprietors dealt with us so calmly, with such dignity that we couldn't give out anymore. They explained it was not their fault. It was the town, *la ville*, that decides those things. What can you say to that? We'd have to go and talk to the town, then. They were like a wall of passivity against our ranting. So we stopped. They didn't shrug once, quite a feat, believe me, in France. It would really have annoyed us if they had.

It was our second time being enclosed in an event and it didn't work out near as well as the day we were imprisoned within the route of the Tour de France in Vendée. We had plans for the afternoon but we couldn't go anywhere. We had no change of clothes. The hotel proprietor drove us to the car later when the fair was over, or nearly over. Even then you couldn't have got through without personal knowledge. He whistled at a man who was directing a tangle of traffic. He said he was the *président* (of the organising committee, I presume. It definitely wasn't President Hollande). He told him we needed to get our car to the hotel. He probably said, in coded language, that we were cantankerous so-and-sos. And the *président* let us through.

We tucked into dinner that evening with extra relish because we had missed lunch. The hotel restaurant was laden with ambience. Ambience is hard to grasp. Everyone knows when it's there but it's impossible to tot up the exact qualities it is composed of.

You had to say the night before if you were not having breakfast, otherwise you would be charged for it. Like ordering dessert in advance, it's not easy to project the state of your appetite a few hours into the future but failure at that particular skill will cost you, because breakfast was not cheap. Declan quipped that as long as they didn't ask us to eat it the night before he didn't mind.

Later in the evening we took a walk around the town. I have to admit the reason we stayed in Montreuil-sur-mer was that it was near to two places we wanted to visit: the Field of the Cloth of Gold and Paris Plage. And when we learned of the historical importance of this town, we felt quite ashamed of ourselves.

Village names ending in euil can claim Celtic links and the *sur mer* (on sea) part of Montreuil gives it links with the sea though it is a distance inland. It was once a thriving seaport, one of the richest in the north and, like Abbeville and a lot of other northern French towns, it was the textile industry that made it. The sea made its way here by the estuary of the Canche River, though it's well silted up now. You can still see the medieval grandeur of the town's past prosperity in the walls and the great rampart.

We walked by the edge of the rampart, though not all three kilometres of it. The view took some beating. The steep drop made the road and railway line look like miniature models. The rounded view of countryside dipped down into a deep valley before it rose again far in the distance, to reach nearly the same height as Montreuil itself. It was a scene like a pastry that turns over the edge of a pie dish.

The rampart looked surprisingly modern, though its last renovations were done by Vauban, Louis XIV's military minister. They could have been done in the last few years for all they have aged. The lower part is in stone and as it reaches towards the top it is in brick, which gives it a fine finish. At intervals there are lookout towers where they once poured boiling tar on anyone who looked suspicious. They were lucky in the hotel that we didn't know about that trick when we arrived tired and cranky.

I'm told that a walk by the rampart's edge when the sun is setting gives off some stunning glows, but there were too many clouds that evening for it to put on its show for us. We walked around the town, up and down cobbled hills, past churches and more churches, closed shops, multi-coloured flowers streaming from old stone buildings.

Treasa saw a nice chair on an antique shop window. "Such a pity it's not open," she said.

I was wondering was she proposing to buy it, and if she was where she thought she might put it.

Declan put words on my thoughts. "You're not suggesting you'd bring that home," he said, half smiling.

"Of course I'm not," she said, a little irritated at his inference.

She dragged herself away with such reluctance that I think maybe that was exactly what she was thinking.

This town used to act as a refuge where people brought valuables for safe keeping in turbulent times. Its rampart was better than the greatest security lock of our age. Modern three-point locking systems, with no facility to throw boiling oil on intruders, pale by comparison. Now Montreuil holds the ambience of the past within it, just as securely as it once held the precious relics and valuables. And to think we only came here because it was near a few places we wanted to see.

Montreuil's more recent history is connected with Victor Hugo. After a brief stop here he made it the setting for *Les Misérables,* which was based on the stormy years of the Napoleonic Empire and the 1830 Revolution. They commemorate it proudly each year, staging an outdoor performance of the work in summer.

# CHAPTER 20

The next day we went looking for the Field of the Cloth of Gold. Famous and all as the meeting was in Tudor history, you would need a search party to find it now. France is a country that could win a prize for good signage, but somehow the skill deserted them here. I have never seen such a network of small roads and tiny villages with so few signs. We didn't even have an address to key into the sat nav. Even Declan conceded defeat. After much trouble we found out that the Field of the Cloth of Gold is located in Balinghem, near Calais. It was hardly surprising that it was so hard to find, because the monument to this event was no more elaborate than a gravestone.

Balinghem was the meeting place of Francis I of France and Henry VIII of England on 7 June 1520. So lavish were their efforts to impress one another – with jousts, banquets, fireworks, pageants and tourneys – that they nearly dazzled each other into bankruptcy. It was a change from war as a foreign policy, but it was costly, something neither of these two insolent kings worried much about. Landing their subjects with the bills of their reckless quests was nothing new. Steve said it was reassuring at least to know that nothing has changed, as far as passing on the expenses of your heady exploits goes; just the actors are different.

What I find to be the biggest coincidence (though Treasa would take issue with me on calling it coincidence) is how two kings so alike as Francis and Henry should have come to the thrones on either side of the channel at the same time. Their lives began within three years of one another and ended within three months. Both were handsome, athletic, flamboyant, indulged, indulgent and absolutely sure of themselves.

When in 1509 the handsome, golden-haired Henry became King of England, not quite eighteen, he was an instant hit with the young. In record time he had emptied the coffers his father had so cautiously built up. The old King had little sense of fun and what price can be put on this shortfall?

Just six years after Henry came to the throne, on the far side of the Channel, the twenty-one-year-old Francis became King of France. A like-minded lover of the jolly side of life, he was a keen patron of the arts. They say he hadn't standard good looks, which you can well believe from Clouet's portraits of him: white skin, narrow eyes and a comically long nose, but he went over well with women. Like Henry, he bled his country dry in his warring quests.

The third member of the European troika was Charles V, who became Holy Roman Emperor, the greatest monarch of his time, at nineteen. He was like a dull addition to the princely pageantry. He was serious, slightly built and pale. He dressed in black and he distanced himself from lively company. He talked little. Steve reckons that people of few words are the most misunderstood of all. "People think because they say little they think equally little, whereas the opposite is true. Because they don't talk much, they've more time to be thoughtful," he said.

Declan said nothing, though I imagine he recognised himself in that description.

Treasa did anyway. "He sounds like you," she said. "You don't believe in saying two words where one word will do."

"He sounds like me?" Declan said in surprise. Then he added with a smile, "I wouldn't mind his inheritance."

Anyway, what Charles lacked in lustre he made up for in political skill and level-headedness. The writer Francis Hackett said of him that even his illegitimate children were conceived with gravity and fortitude.

We couldn't stay long in the Field of the Cloth of Gold. There wasn't even a space to park a car while you read the inscription on

153

the marble memorial that recalls this event. That's amazing, because in France they provide car-parks for the most run-of-the-mill things. The memorial is certainly out of line with the glitter of the event. I've seen bigger tombstones on the resting place of the most ordinary folk.

The man who convened the meeting on the Field of the Cloth of Gold was Cardinal Wolsey, the chief minister and effective ruler of England, someone who knew a thing or two about the benefit of theatre (his court rivalled that of the Tudors'). The site of the meeting was an English possession, part of the limited territory England still held in France, and the French King agreed to meet on conquered soil, putting him rather on the back foot. Each camp took up about a hectare of field. Thousands of silken tents were erected. Francis ordered that his be made with cloth of gold, with apples of gold crowned by a gold Saint Michael.

The English had done their preparatory work well. They built a windowed palace at home – a replica of the guildhall in Calais – shipped it to France in sections and put it together in a quick assembly job that would give Ikea a run for its money.

A pavilion served as a chapel, another as a great hall where colourful tapestries were hung and gilt fountains spewed out claret, spiced wine and water. The French tent was not up to the stress of this breezy part of the country and it blew over. But Francis's women in their elegant fabric and precious gems, made up for the lesser substance of the tents.

Francis's wife, Queen Claude, was there, his mother, Louise and his sister, Marguerite. His mistress was brought along too. Virtually all the English court crossed the Channel for the event: Henry's wife, Catherine of Aragon (aunt of Charles V), Mary Tudor, former Queen of France and a host of others, though not the king's mistress. To bring the King's mistress into full view might have been accepted in France (that kind of liberty is thought to date back to the troubadours) but not in England. The thing was that the King was allowed a dual love life, an official wife to ensure the right lineage, and a mistress to make up for such marital sacrifice. Without this double arrangement he might have to marry outside and import common blood into the royal house. Perish the thought.

"There was very little social variety to that, insisting that royal blood stayed in royal blood," said Treasa.

"Ah well, the poor could provide the variety," said Declan.

Not until Anne Boleyn came on the scene, six or seven years after this famous meeting in Balinghem, did the English King's mistress come into full public view. And in any case he married her, so it was different. King Francis never approved of the Boleyn marriage. She was not welcome at the French court. Her blood lines weren't up to it.

That day in Balinghem Charles V let the two kings revel in partying to their hearts' content and when all the merriment was over, he went on with the English to Calais. Francis lingered around Boulogne hoping to get an invite to the ball in Calais, where the English were entertaining the Holy Roman Emperor, but none came.

No trace of this burst of energy remains in these parts now. The only sign of gold in Balinghem that day was the corn that swayed in the lively breeze.

Just one place remained to see: Le Touquet-Paris-Plage. When I first saw the road-sign for this seaside resort I thought it was a remnant of the past, a museum beach where Parisians went before the ease of travel lured them all southwards. So it came as a surprise to find the place was thriving, so much so that we could hardly move in the traffic. While we were at a standstill we caught glimpses of the forests and villas for which the place is known. They were half concealed by the long-legged trees and they peeped out of their hideouts like something from a fairy tale.

This place is said to have been the most elegant holiday resort of northern France, "the playground of rich Parisians", and that claim ties in with the popular lore of the late nineteenth century when it was established. It was the brainchild of Hippolyte de Villemessant, founder of *Le Figaro* newspaper and other publications. The idea struck him one day as he hunted with his friend Jean-Baptiste Daloz on the Daloz estate that this would be the perfect place for a *station balnéaire* (a seaside resort). And so a thousand hectares of forest capped by a beach of brilliant white was set aside for this business venture.

It would be hard to find a better place. The shoreline goes on glowingly as far as the eye can see. The sand looks as if it has been put through the finest of sieves. I reckon you could search the whole expanse of beach of Le Touquet-Paris-Plage, in vain, to find a single stone to hold down a corner of your towel. The day we visited, the water was a great distance out into the English Channel – *La Manche*. You would have to be eager for a swim, because to find enough depth would entail a long walk. Steve said to get as far as the water we could rent one of the children's trikes which were available on the seafront at €2.00 for ten minutes.

We had planned to walk to the end of the beach, but we changed our minds because the wind was strong and the fine sand was blowing in our eyes, so in the end our stroll was a lot more modest. The flying sand was not bothering the children who formed long queues for the carousels, swings and slides along the seafront, however. The generous spread of amusements looked out of step with the care that was taken with this town in the past.

Strict control was put on building design here in the late nineteenth and early twentieth centuries and you can well see the result. Apart from a few modern tatty-looking buildings on the seafront, the town is a model of grid-like order. Houses with timber balconies and outside banisters painted in delicate shades are the picture of symmetry.

In the roaring twenties Le Touquet-Paris-Plage was a popular outpost for rich English visitors, the so-called smart set (the English coast is just seventy miles away). Some hotel names – Bristol Hotel, Westminster Hotel – recall that English link. It was a much loved spot of the English playwright Noel Coward and of the high society, the theme of many of his plays, who descended here in real life at weekends. Their legacy is visible in some of the showy villas that peep out of the woods. We took a trip around in the *train touristique*. Nowhere was it more needed, because it is a sprawl of a place and parking is as difficult here as in any big city centre.

When we came back to Montreuil-sur-mer that evening, we parked in a spot that would be easy to get out of at an early hour the following morning. While the town's old and narrow streets are delightful, we wouldn't have been so taken by them in the morning if we were hemmed in by some late-night straggler who decided he was the last home. People are a little haphazard about parking rules in this town.

We were going to go to bed in good time to make up for our early morning rise, but as with ordering dessert or breakfast before hunger strikes you, to sleep before the urge comes is not the easiest of things to do. Declan suggested a game of Scrabble to relax everyone. That, as it happened, did anything but, because of the amount of arguing about words. Treasa is exact about scrabble and Steve was putting her endurance to the test, coming up with the most original of spellings so we decided to abandon the game and read instead.

# CHAPTER 21

Next morning we treaded softly to the car lest we waken the giant morning out of its slumber. We had done a practice run the evening before out of Montreuil-sur-mer, to make sure we knew the one-way system. Steve said we couldn't afford to make a mistake now that there was no presidential election coming up. He was having a joke on the comical French custom of an amnesty doled out by a newly elected president. A presidential pardon for small offences was begun by de Gaulle which was not too unlike the medieval French King's power to heal by his touch.

The result is that carelessness is noticeable coming up to a presidential election. Drivers ignore red lights, park wherever it suits them, break speed limits. So a new president allows you to break the law at your ease, though this quaint practice is a lot less generous than it used to be.

Day was breaking as we left. Dew hung in the air. Early morning mystery pulsated. It was that time of day when the light doesn't know whether it is day or night. With the road to ourselves, we were quickly out of town. Changing landscapes sped by, gentle hills rising and dipping, starry villages still sleeping with their full lights on. Their photo sensors had not yet been given the signal that it was day. Fog rose like steam out of the depth of valleys. Fields reacted to the morning in their own way. The untilled pastures held on to their covering of morning dew, like bashful maidens shielding themselves beneath their veils. No cloak of haze hung over the cornfields. They glowed and flowed, showing off their golden tresses and wagging their rumps like brazen hussies, to the god of dawn.

There were few cars on the road. No delays. The red-roofed and neatly built houses of Calais were soon in sight. French houses look small but they can be deceptive. They have a habit of building upwards and downwards rather than outwards, a preference for discretion, with eyebrow windows built into the roof and cellars dug into the ground. Older houses are built in stone; newer ones go for plastered exteriors. Red brick is rare. Discretion of design does not apply to the church in every village, however. Towering and arrow-like their spires looked as severe as the punishment that went with transgression.

We had reached our port of departure, panic over, no unexpected hold-ups. We took our place in the queue. People were drinking coffee. Some had brought flasks. Accents were different now. It was like a patch of England on French soil. You picked out the northern from the southern or western English inflections and further north into Scotland. I've never heard an Irish accent on the Calais-Dover run, save our own.

Some French conversations were audible. They were beginning their holiday. It felt strange. Even though we had had a great time, I wouldn't have swapped with them. It's a mindset, this idea of coming and going, beginning and ending. It is like wanting to relive your life. Would you do it all over again? Steve says he would like to go back to thirty and stay there forever.

"Why thirty?" asked Treasa.

"Why not thirty?" he explained.

Declan says those things are not available so why bother even discussing them. It was hard to disagree with that, especially at that hour of the morning. I felt like asking them to give up their juvenile discussion.

Treasa kept it going: "Look at all Cesare Borgia or King Francis had achieved by thirty," she said.

"Yes indeed, and think of how they travelled too. They didn't move much slower than the mode of transport we chose to come by. Think about how fast this would all have been by plane," said Declan.

The vessel was loaded. It had taken all the cargo its belly could hold. Vehicles were packed tightly, buses emptied; their passengers had taken to the decks. Trucks were full of their carefully packed merchandise, cars held roof boxes stacked to maximum height, containing everything from the practical to the retail folly, the kind of thing that makes you wonder for the rest of the year, whatever did you buy that for. What the impulse of holidays has to answer for. At least we didn't have the chair Treasa had been eyeing up in Montreuil-sur-mer.

The bow doors were secured and we were ready to face the sea. The boat swayed as it turned itself like an awkward animal moves in his lair. With its rump to land it chugged out of the port. Starry and flickering Calais moved into retreat. Everyone agrees there's a magic about this hour of day, even late sleepers who experience it grudgingly. Passengers twisted and turned on their seats to find a comfortable position. A seat is no substitute for a bed. Some tried to make up for the absence by occupying two or three seats, even though they were asked not to. But they didn't look as if they cared. Their heads nodded and tumbled in semi-consciousness. Mouths hung open. Some placed their grimy shoes where others were going to have to sit. I hoped it wouldn't be fussy Treasa in her immaculate clothes. Even on a ferry she dresses beautifully.

The coastal strip of northern France floated by, sandy beaches glowed white as they lay empty, untrampled on at this cold hour of day. The growing light made the coastline more visible. Lighthouses on the finger tips of land still beamed in careful sequence, standing watch lest their help be needed to point out the danger spots. A boat lit up in the morning sun, lone and distant against the sky.

Safety instructions spoke loudly.

"No matter how many times you hear them I bet you still couldn't put on a life jacket or find the whistle to blow to signal that you're in trouble without looking up the instructions," said Steve.

"And in a real life emergency you probably wouldn't be able to read at all because the words would jump before your eyes," replied Treasa.

"But I think the whistle idea is the funniest of all," he said. "Exactly who would you expect to hear you? The person alongside you, probably, and they'd be in equal trouble."

There was a crowd of teenagers on the boat. They were noisy and giddy with youth. Girls linked in friendship were singing, yes singing at this hour of the morning. How inconsiderate to be in such good humour, getting on the nerves of grumpy adults who had long lost that exuberance. I wasn't much older than they when I took off on my own to Paris with a single address, when life looked so dreamy that it didn't have to be planned as far as sundown. They were taking photos on phones, then shrieking with laughter when they viewed the reproduction of themselves. It was as if they had no idea until then what they looked like. They will gaze at these pictures in years to come and wonder who in the name of goodness those people were. That is if these snapshots ever reach hard copy status.

The sky glowed red. Then the red streaks curdled, as if the oil of day had been added too quickly to the emulsion. The sun peeped its yellow head over the rim of earth, cautiously observing the world it had woken up. As it pushed out into visibility, it changed colour from paler to more full-blooded orangey hues. And just before the sea gave it its final push into birth, it formed a reflection in the water, a double self, a moment of contemplation before it left the safe womb of ocean. The sky changed shade like zillions of angels arrayed in varying shades of blue, silently worshipping the birth of day. And then the sun went on its independent way. As it soars high and bright into the heights of day, it loses its hold on you, like the novelty wears off the newborn. Not until evening, when it dips again towards the horizon will it bring the world to a halt, to gaze as it sets in a display of brilliance. Like birth and death hold the interest more than the daily course of life.

Declan was reading, a magazine, not a map. An Englishman had got into conversation with Steve. He was telling him his life story: his ex wife, his children, his cooking skills, the friends he had visited in France, the great coincidence of how he made friends with them

161

in the first place. Where are you Treasa when we need you, to put him right on that one, that there's no such thing as coincidence? Her gaze was fixed on the sea, watching the seabirds as they flew low, ready to pounce on whatever prey showed its unlucky head beneath the waters. The waves were putting on a nice show. As they broke on the water's surface they swirled, frothed and foamed like horses panting and fuming to win a race, only to be beaten by the great sea taking them in folds into its interiors. Nifty scrabble words were flooding into my head. They were pretty restrained in the hotel the evening before when I needed them.

It had been a great holiday. Sure, there were the sulks and silences, when vows of "never again" were taken. But they were quickly forgotten, neutralised by the moments of sheer joy – of pure presence – that can only be felt when you're out of routine, beyond the daily grind that so dulls real joy. Our boundaries merged at times, like wet paint flows over its allotted area. We had shared qualities, although I doubt if Declan acquired Treasa's romantic outlook or that she took on any of his technical skills. Steve's happy-go-lucky disposition had the best transferring power of all. His good humour shamed the rest of us into being a bit more jolly. I never found out what I brought to the group and I never asked.